D1356958

H46 562 798 5

...The First Lady of
BOND......

...The First Lady of
BOND.....

Eunice Gayson

with **Andrew Boyle and Gareth Owen**

SIGNUM BOOKS

First published in Great Britain in 2012 by Signum Books
an imprint of
Flashpoint Media Ltd
22 Signet Court
Cambridge
CB5 8LA

A CIP catalogue record for this book is
available from the British Library.

ISBN 978 0 9566534 7 5

Edited by Marcus Hearn
Designed by Peri Godbold

Printed and bound in China by 1010 Printing International Ltd.

Contents

Acknowledgements

Firstly, my thanks must go to Andrew Boyle and Gareth Owen for all their help, research and guidance in producing this book. Also to my publisher Marcus Hearn for being so enthusiastic, helpful and supportive throughout the whole process.

My thanks, too, to Barbara Broccoli, Meg Simmonds and everyone at Eon Productions for their kind help and permission to reproduce images from the James Bond Films.

And a big thank you to Sir Roger Moore for writing such a kind introduction and for being a super actor to work with.

I'm also grateful to Iris 'Eagle Eye' Harwood, Bert Fink (Rodgers and Hammerstein: an Imagem Company), the BBC Written Archive, Mark Mawston, Jaz Wiseman (www.itc-classics.com), Jonathan Rigby, Marc Pearce, Irene Estry, Euan Lloyd, the TCM Classic Film Festival (Turner Broadcasting System Inc), Derek Pykett, Kate Gayson, John Murray, Dave Worrall and Lee Pfeiffer of Cinema Retro (www.cinemaretro.com), Nigel Trigwell, the National Motor Museum at Beaulieu, Janet Benney (née Edwardes), Göran Krantz, and Robin Harbour – the West Midlands' biggest collector of James Bond memorabilia.

Foreword

I first met Eunice when I was a struggling young actor in the 1950s. I'd be sitting in the outer office with a bunch of other hungry hopefuls, waiting to be called, and Eunice would arrive, smile and say a cheery 'Hello' to everyone before being whisked straight in, as she invariably knew the director or producer. I'm only glad we were never up for the same parts as I wouldn't have stood a chance!

Though we met socially, and in particular with Diana Dors, it wasn't until I started filming *The Saint* in the 1960s that I had the opportunity to work with Eunice – on two episodes in fact – and it was huge fun. Around seven or eight years ago we got together to record a DVD commentary for one of the episodes and it was as though the intervening decades had never occurred.

Alas, I never made a Bond film with Eunice; you see, her character only had eyes for Sean.

I'm so pleased Eunice has now decided to write a memoir, and am delighted to have been asked to pen a few words to open it.

Roger Moore

CHAPTER ONE

Childhood Years

S t Patrick's Day, 17 March 1928, arrived and so did I – bang on time. And I've been just as punctual ever since!

Of course my parents were expecting just the one baby. So when my mother told the doctor there was most definitely another one on the way out, he was just as surprised as everyone else. Imagine the delight when 20 minutes later my darling twin sister Patricia was born. The young doctor was overwhelmed, as this was his first ever twin birth. Yes, I am a twin, and it has brought me much joy and happiness throughout my life. Pat was much smaller than me and had dark hair, whereas I was a blonde-haired baby and didn't go dark until after a childhood bout of scarlet fever.

My mother was naturally overjoyed with her two bouncing baby daughters, but Father was not so sure as he wanted another son. Our brother Kenneth, who was nine years older than us, was apparently also horrified to learn that he wasn't getting a baby brother but a sister – what's more, not one but two. 'One girl is bad enough, but two is disgusting,' he was heard to say. Initially he wanted nothing to do with the new arrivals, but slowly and surely he came round and became absolutely besotted with us.

My mother, Maria, came from an English family of five sisters and two brothers (both of whom sadly died in the First World War) and was one of the most beautiful women I have ever known. Not only did beauty radiate from her peach-like complexion – in fact she earned the nickname Billie the Peach – but it shone from deep within too.

She had an incredibly positive 'have a go' attitude which, looking back, rubbed off on all three of her children. She was also highly intelligent and had amazing mathematical abilities; for example, she could add up huge lists of numbers in her head in seconds. Before marrying my father she put her skills to good use working as one of the first female bank tellers in the UK. She was also very good at calligraphy, and even a note to the milkman was written in the most beautiful handwriting imaginable.

My father John, on the other hand, was a complete enigma to us all. He was of French-Irish descent, and Mother married him on the rebound after ending a previous engagement – which, in hindsight, wasn't perhaps the best basis for a successful marriage. By all accounts, my mother had been engaged to C J Lytle, who was very prominent in the world of publicity and PR. She said Lytle was due to go abroad to Rio de Janeiro, indefinitely; she didn't fancy that, so the engagement was called off. She then met my father and married him instead, despite them having very little in common.

In fact, their personalities were polar opposites, with my father being rather cold, distant and controlling. He was educated at a boys' private school in Ireland which was run by his father, my grandfather, who ensured his four sons were all exemplary pupils and excelled academically through hard study and long hours. I fear Father's academic excellence – which included being fluent in French, German and Mandarin Chinese – came at the cost of his childhood, and this obviously affected him for the rest of his life.

No one, not even my mother, knew anything about my father's early career. Before we were born they had lived for a while in China and France, where, he said, he held 'administrative positions'. Later on, back in London, I remember coming home to find my father had returned from one of his overseas trips. When

Childhood Years

I innocently asked where he had been, my mother told me to 'Shhh' and my father raised his hand, as if to say: 'I don't want to talk about it.'

As a result we never really got to know our father at all, and only after he died did our mother admit she suspected he was a spy working for the British government. His personality certainly would have suited that.

My early childhood memories are sketchy as we always seemed to be on the move. One thing I know for sure was that my name was set in stone. A family tradition, spanning hundreds of years, stated that the first-born girl in the family should be named Eunice (from the Greek Euníkē, 'Eu' meaning good and 'níkē', victory). Our family name, Sargaison, had French origins. My father was set on breaking this tradition, because as I've mentioned he had wanted a second son and this was his way of being awkward – one of his many traits. He decided I should be named Patricia and my sister (the second-born in this case) Eunice. It was only when a mix-up occurred at the christening, and I was mistakenly named Eunice, that my mother was finally able to overrule Father's decision.

As in the womb, Pat and I were inseparable throughout our lives; as very young children, I remember we spent hours on end in our double pram holding hands, rocking backwards and forwards and screaming with laughter. We couldn't talk then, but we had a way of communicating and seemed to know what the other was thinking. It's hard to explain, and difficult to understand unless you are a twin.

My first memory of home is of us all living in a large Victorian house in Streatham, south London. Pat and I had taken our first steps there, and became quite confident little walkers in fact. One day we decided to go on an adventure all of our own. Mother had been gardening and had left her muddy shoes near the porch, so I slipped into one and my sister into the other. They were pretty heavy shoes and quite difficult to walk in but nothing was going to stop us. Off we toddled. Our house was situated on a very steep hill and we obviously decided it would be exciting to walk right down to the bottom. It was a very busy road and we had absolutely no sense of danger whatsoever; cars apparently came screeching to a halt with their horns blaring, people were waving and shouting. But did we care? Quite frankly, no!

Mother heard all the commotion outside and went to see what was causing it, little realising it was her own daughters. We must have been three-quarters of the way down the hill before our mother caught up with us, screaming 'STOP THEM!' When we got home Father was waiting for us.

'Eunice, Patricia, what have you been doing?' he bellowed.

Father always called us by our pet names – I was Mimi and Patricia was Lulu. So we knew if he used our real names we were in *big* trouble.

We actually got some publicity from our little adventure, when a photograph of us wearing gardening shoes was published in the local newspaper. My first taste of stardom, perhaps!

Shortly afterwards, a children's shoe manufacturer, Start-rite, produced a very successful advertising campaign featuring, yes, you guessed it, two cute kids arm-in-arm walking into the distance, with one foot each in a pair of grown-up shoes. My mother swore it was based on the picture published in our local paper.

To Purley

My mother became unhappy in Streatham. She said it wasn't a particularly nice area to live in any more – especially with a young family – and, besides which, since Pat and I arrived things were getting a little cramped in the house. So she decided we'd be better off moving to Purley, Surrey, an area she'd often visited and liked hugely. My father, who just wanted an easy life, was more than happy for others to make the household decisions and went along with whatever had been decided. I remember moving into a large detached house with a massive garden, all lined with trees; oh, there was a pond too, with fish. I really loved that house and have so many happy memories of it and my formative years there.

Sadly my maternal Grandmother died shortly before our move. She was a dear little lady and quite probably the most cuddlesome person that was ever born. She was widowed at a relatively young age, and left to fend for herself; there was no state assistance back then, so she had to work. She became very interested in the property market. In fact she was always moving, buying up wrecks of houses to refurbish. It was, I must admit, a highly unusual occupation for a lady in that period, but she made such a huge success of it that she was able to privately educate all her children to a high standard, enjoy a comfortable lifestyle, and leave a sizable inheritance when she died. There was certainly a lot of ingenuity in my family, which thankfully rubbed off on me a bit too.

My brother Kenny left school when we were still quite young, and worked as a fledgling journalist in Fleet Street by day and, by night, locked himself away in his bedroom, poring over any film books and magazines he could get his hands on. He was a real cinema buff and his bedroom walls were covered with pictures and posters of his favourite stars; there wasn't an actor or director he didn't know of and he hoped one day to work his way up the journalistic ladder to become a film critic.

My father, of course, had different ideas and decided banking would be a more appropriate profession for his only son. Kenny, however, had very little interest in it. Over the months, and indeed years, my brother began to resent my father. Not once did Father ever praise him for the articles he wrote, nor did he ever encourage Kenny, aside from his suggestions of packing it in and becoming a banker, and I know Kenny just wanted to escape the stifling home environment.

It all came to a head after an incident in which Kenny launched a model plane through the stained glass window of the local church, much to the chagrin of the vicar. My father hit the roof, as he had to pay for a new window, and shouted furiously: 'How can you be so useless and pathetic? I want you out of this house.'

They were very harsh and unfair words, but words Father meant; he felt his son was a disappointment. Kenny took Father's advice literally. In fact, not only did he leave the house but also the country. He was just 17 years old.

We had a huge extended family with relatives scattered all over the world, so choosing somewhere to start his new life with familiar faces around wasn't going to be that difficult. But Kenny's message to Father couldn't have been stronger: he was emigrating to Australia.

Mother took the news badly, as did Pat and me, but Father showed no regret at all. Even when our mother arranged a send-off bash at the house in Purley – inviting relatives from all over, all of whom masked their devastation with feigned happiness and good wishes – Father barely showed his face.

Initially, Kenny worked on the cattle ranch belonging to my Aunt Grace (Mother's sister), then moved on to head the Australian Film Unit during the Second World War. There he combined his two loves of journalism and film.

After the war he asked what was going to happen to all the unit's fantastic state-of-the-art equipment – cameras, projectors, sound recorders, screens – you name it. He was told the Australian government were just going to 'dispose' of it all. Thinking that was quite ridiculous, he said 'Can I have it?' Amazingly, they said 'Certainly.' So Kenny decided he would open a cinema (maybe even a small chain). But then reports came back that the boat carrying all his equipment around the coast had sunk – though

Kenny believed the gear had actually been stolen. He then made a bit of a sideways move and became a radio DJ and, later on, a salesman. Life was good to Kenny in Australia, where he married and became father to five adorable children.

Pat's accident

Back in England, during the school holidays, rather than getting under my mother's feet, my eight-year-old sister and I were bustled off to Miss Minter's Summer School in Westcliff-on-Sea, Essex. It was an adventure we both looked forward to greatly; our days were spent walking, swimming and playing on the beach. The evenings were fun too. After Matron had done her rounds we'd make ropes out of our bed sheets and shimmy down from our rooms, and then onto the beach to meet the boys from the local school! There we spent wonderful times, eating stale sandwiches and dancing the night away before creeping home in the early hours before Matron did her rounds again. We were never really interested in boys in 'that way' but it was a lot of fun and we felt like liberated grown-ups.

One particular day there, our lives changed forever.

Slow dissolve…

The path down to the seashore was very steep and narrow so we'd all be marched down single file. I was always at the front of the group and Pat usually followed right behind, but on this occasion she'd obviously found something interesting to look at and was trailing at the back. All of a sudden our happy chattering was shattered by an almighty scream. I turned around and saw my sister lying on the ground crying. Apparently, the local delivery boy had been trying to show off by following us down the hill on his bike but had lost control, ploughing directly into the back of the group and knocking my sister over. Thankfully, she wasn't too badly hurt; in fact, it was more a shock than anything else. After a few cuts and bruises had been tended to, the teacher suggested a nice swim would be just what the doctor ordered, and we all continued on our merry way.

Later that night, while lying in bed, I heard a strange muttering and moaning sound from my sister's bed. Glancing over I was shocked to see her absolutely dripping in sweat, terribly, terribly pale and in a semi-conscious state. I screamed for the Matron, who immediately called an ambulance and Pat was rushed straight to hospital.

My mother tore down from Purley – as usual, Father was away on one of his mysterious trips – and after a few tense days at her bedside we were given the terrible news that Patricia had contracted osteomyelitis of the hip. The doctor said that swimming in the sea with open wounds, along with the trauma from her recent accident, was the likely cause. Her condition, the doctor explained, involved a *severely* infected bone which, along with intense pain, usually led to arthritis and reduced limb and joint function. In fact, we were told that not only would Pat never leave hospital but that she'd never walk again. Back then, very little was known about this debilitating condition and, until the introduction of modern antibiotics, there was no cure.

Upon hearing the news, my father said the most hurtful thing imaginable:

'Oh, if only it had happened to you, Eunice.'

'Why?' I asked.

'Well, you are so much bigger and stronger than Patricia and would have just shrugged it off.'

This gave me an incredible complex. How could any father wish that upon his child? For ever after I felt incredibly guilty taking part in any kind of physical activity, knowing that my poor sister couldn't walk and that my own father wished it was me lying there instead.

Childhood Years

Pat's illness alone was hugely cruel. It had always been thought she would one day become a professional dancer. She could do anything with her body, but now all those dreams had been shattered – and all through a simple accident. It was so unfair and effectively ended her life as we all knew it.

For weeks and months Pat was in complete isolation in Purley Hospital, and I was forbidden to visit her. It was absolutely heart-breaking, as we'd spent virtually every day of our young lives together. But now, at the doctor's insistence in the hope her condition would improve, the only contact I was allowed was waving through holes I'd cut in the hedge outside her window. I'd catch her eye and she'd smile and wave, all the time lying on her back with one leg suspended on a pulley. She was an incredibly brave soul who, despite her situation, never complained – a true inspiration to me.

With my brother in Australia and my sister in hospital I felt totally alone. For solace I spent hours indulging in what became my two great passions in life: music and literature. My mother, bless her heart, bought me wonderful 78 rpm records featuring the popular singers of the time such as Jussi Björling, Beniamino Gigli and Elisabeth Schwarzkopf performing the most beautiful arias. I'd just drift away, imagining one day I would be able to sing as well. I also accumulated a huge library of books and spent hours reading; in fact, I had so many that during the war I rented them out and donated the money to the Red Cross!

We'd lived in Purley for quite a few years when World War II broke out. Father announced, partly owing to his job and partly to escape the Blitz, that we'd be relocating to Glasgow, Clarkston to be exact. Mother and I were forbidden to ask the whys and wherefores, and, despite the fact that his announcement clearly upset me, Father showed no interest in our apprehension about moving to the other end of the country. As far as he was concerned, that was that.

By this time, Pat had been isolated in hospital for over a year. Mother had been allowed to visit under strict hygiene conditions, and carried messages to and from Pat and other members of the family, none of whom were allowed to visit – myself included.

The doctors showed no signs of letting Pat come home; they protested her condition would only improve under their care. But she'd been in their care a year already! Mother took matters into her own hands and demanded her release, saying 'Without Patricia we can't move to Scotland, and to safety away from the bombings.' With the mass evacuation of children from London and its suburbs underway, they agreed, albeit reluctantly, as long as Pat's treatment could continue after we'd moved. Mother gave them every assurance and signed every paper they asked for.

'At last!' I thought. 'My darling sister is coming home.'

It was then my dear Aunt Eunice intervened and suggested my sister and I sail to the safety of New York instead, where Pat could get the best medical treatment. She pressed ahead and made the initial travel plans. Though the adventure sounded fun, I wasn't keen on moving even further away and leaving my mother behind. Although Mother kept telling us it was for the best, as the departure date drew nearer it became clear she simply couldn't bear to be parted from her daughters; our trip was cancelled. Call it fate if you will, but the ship we were booked on was sunk by a U-boat during its Atlantic crossing. All lives were lost.

My Aunt Eunice, I should explain, was English but had married an American and moved out there. There was a huge fashion store in London's Regent Street called Marshall and Snelgrove, and Aunt Eunice was the head of the linen department. She was so beautiful, and brilliant at business too; a real sharp cookie. One day an American multi-millionaire went in to buy some linen for his yacht and fell madly in love with my Aunt Eunice on the spot – as did most of her customers.

Childhood Years

Apparently he said, 'You're going to marry me.' To which she replied, 'Yes sir, which of these would you like?'

He was staying in a huge suite at the Savoy Hotel, where the linen was delivered to, and went back to Marshall's every single day for a week, just so he could see my Aunt Eunice and pronounce his love. Eventually he wore her down and they fell madly in love. They married soon afterwards and he became my Uncle Lewis. He swept her off to live with him in New York where he worked as a banker and as one of the original developers of Coney Island.

Anyhow, I digress. The day of the move to Scotland arrived. Both my mother and father owned cars, as with Father away so much it was felt Mother should be mobile too. I remember feeling so sad, seeing all our belongings jammed into the back, ready for the long journey that was ahead of us. I felt I had to say one last goodbye to my beloved bedroom and went back inside. My mother and Pat had already started off on the long trek north, and as I walked over to the window I saw my father driving off into the distance. He'd assumed I was with my mother and Pat in their car.

I burst into tears.

I thought the best thing to do would be to just sit and wait. They'd surely meet at some point and realise they'd left me behind, wouldn't they? Minutes turned to hours and as night fell I became really frightened. There was no light or heat as both the gas and electricity had been turned off, so I huddled on the stairs and to occupy my mind began to sing.

My voice echoed through the empty house and I remember thinking to myself 'Hey, I like this.' With the moonlight acting as a makeshift spotlight, I belted out a favourite song from one of my beloved records and felt transported to another place.

All of a sudden there was a screech of brakes and the front door flew open. My parents rushed in, devastated that they'd left me behind, and found me sitting on the stairs smiling widely and looking totally content with myself.

'Are you OK, Eunice?' my mother asked as she grabbed me.

'Yes mummy. I can sing!'

Scotland bound

The move to Glasgow meant starting a new school. I certainly got the impression there was a lot of anti-English feeling at the time. Whenever I walked into a classroom there'd be something scrawled on the inside of my desk, such as 'Go home, you dirty Sassenach.'

It was strange because, in time, I made a lot of good friends and could never quite work out who continued to write such nastiness on an almost daily basis, though I suspected everyone. What's more, I was always marked down in exams – in subjects which I normally excelled in – and I think this was the only time my father ever stood up for me. He went down to the school and asked the teachers why my marks were low, and they would always say 'Oh, it must be exam nerves.' He dismissed that as 'absolute rubbish' and made his 'concern' known to them.

I think the locals resented the fact that we'd seemingly moved to Glasgow only to escape the bombing raids on London, which is ironic, as no sooner had we arrived than the Clydeside docks area suffered incredible damage from the Luftwaffe. I always remember scrambling under a huge oak table in our house as the air raid sirens and the drone of the German heavy bombers filled the air, on their way to drop their deadly loads on the Scottish shipyards and munitions factories. It's a sound that haunted me for many years afterwards, as did the sight of bullet holes in my bedroom wall one morning after a raid. That was a bit too close for comfort.

Through all this, however, the resentful locals never knew the real reason we'd moved there, a reason that unfolded many years later after my father died. Keep reading!

Childhood Years

Father had passed off my 'solo spot' at the old house in Purley as a childish phase. Mother, on the other hand, obviously saw potential and arranged singing lessons with a renowned teacher, Patrick Guilfoyle, who used to sing at the world-famous La Scala Opera House in Milan. I was instructed by Mother that under no circumstances should I tell my father as he would be 'absolutely furious and we'd both end up in trouble.' Fortunately, he was always 'away on business' and it was fairly easy to get away with our little secret.

Not content with just organising singing lessons, my mother encouraged my artistic leanings by entering me into every talent competition going. As well as singing I often performed tap, delivered little monologues or recited poetry. I usually ended up winning, too! As a result I happily landed a few guest roles (glorified cameos really) in shows at various theatres in Glasgow, which in turn led to my first ever professional gig.

Patrick Guilfoyle lived and worked in Paisley and had connections with the Logan acting family. Ella Logan was a singer and actress who later became extremely successful in many Broadway shows, while her nephew Jimmy Logan – whose parents were the music hall act Short and Dalziel – became an accomplished actor and director, probably best remembered for his appearances in the Carry On films and TV shows like *Rab C Nesbitt*. But back then, Jimmy helped run the family-owned theatre.

Patrick knew they were always on the lookout for variety acts and he suggested I go along to amateur night to show-off my abilities. I performed 'Alice Blue Gown' and stole the show. Along with it I netted the top prize of £5. The crowd called for an encore, which was impossible as I'd not learnt anything else!

They asked me if I'd go back the next week, and so my mother bought me a lovely new dress and, armed with a few more songs, I won the second week as well. I was then offered a week-long

engagement for the princely sum of £25. It was my very first paid
job and a real thrill.

The Logans then asked me to audition for the role of a fairy in
their annual pantomime. Not wanting to miss any opportunity
I readily agreed. But there was a slight problem; the fairy was a
ballerina. I'd never done ballet in my life but, with my mother's
cavalier 'have a go' attitude instilled in me, I thought 'What the
hell, how hard can it be?'

My mother bought me a pair of ballet shoes and I went along
to the audition. When they asked me if I could do point work
I nervously said 'Yes.' I went up on my toes and it was absolute
agony! Apparently it can take years for the toes to harden and
if I got the job I knew I'd be doing this twice a day for at least
two weeks.

When they told me I'd landed the part I didn't know whether to
laugh or cry. But I remembered my dear sister, who'd never get her
chance, and from that moment on I just got on with it and never
complained. That's showbusiness, isn't it?

As I think I've made clear, my father had very little in the
way of compassion when it came to his children. Kenny was
far enough away not to concern him of course, but his coldness
towards me was further demonstrated when I had a nasty
accident at school. My arm was scalded very badly with boiling
water and I was rushed to hospital with awful blisters and burns.
I later returned home with my mother, bandaged up like an
Egyptian mummy, just in time for dinner, and there was Father
sitting at the table. I waited for him to react, but he never uttered
a single word.

'Aren't you ever going to ask?' I eventually enquired.

'What do you mean?'

'Can't you see I've been hurt? Oh daddy just, forget it!' I cried.

I think my father found it hard to show any kind of emotion
because of his strict upbringing. One thing he did do, though, was

bottle it up until he just couldn't hold back, and would then rant and rave; just like now.

'How dare a daughter of mine speak to me in such a manner and show so little respect?' he snapped.

He went on about working hard to provide us with a nice home, and so on, and on and on. When he eventually finished telling me how grateful I should be, I told him I thought he was 'very uncaring' and ran up to my room.

Pat would always hug me and tell me not to worry. How she remained so compassionate and understanding I'll never know. Her life was a daily battle against disability, and back then being disabled was not something easily accepted by others. There'd be mumblings of 'the cripple girl' from people, as if Pat was some sort of lesser mortal, and to my mind it was the worst form of prejudice.

Sir Thomas

In 1942 I read an article by the English conductor and impresario Sir Thomas Beecham, who, it seemed, had a disregard for English female opera singers, saying they 'lacked drive, warmth and passion' and if the profession was to survive 'they would have to import singers from other countries.' This irked me somewhat; I therefore decided to write to him, asking his advice as to whether my voice was good enough for me to become a professional singer. Well, what did I have to lose?

I waited day after day for a reply, but it never came. After a year I'd forgotten about it when, to my total surprise, Dr Berta Geissmar, Sir Thomas's Major-domo, replied, inviting me to sing for the Maestro in Liverpool, where he was conducting at the time. It was a great privilege when Sir Thomas decided to accompany me on the piano while I sang Butterfly's Entrance from *Madam Butterfly* – terrifying, but madly exciting and thrilling. It was an experience I'll never forget.

Sir Thomas seemed impressed with my performance and suggested I continue with my education and voice coaching, after which I should see him again with a view to training under him. With war still raging and being so far from London, Father said it was difficult to plan so far ahead and that was that.

It wasn't long after this when Father announced that, due to his work, we'd be moving to Edinburgh.

'Not again!' I thought.

Well, at least it wasn't, relatively speaking, a move to the other end of the country, though of course it meant moving to yet another school, and making new friends. But thankfully that was a skill I was really beginning to master.

I enrolled at the Edinburgh Academy.

Mother always continued to encourage my artistic side and I remember Christmas being a lot of fun in our house. Father would rarely be at home and Mother would let me write a family show, with me playing the lead of course. We had relatives join us from all over, and all said 'One day you'll make it in show business, Eunice.' It was an encouragement I yearned to hear from my father, but I realised it would never come.

In fact, the only time I ever recall my father watching me perform was at the Usher Hall in Edinburgh. I'd finished my short set and was heading off stage when the house lights came up early, and as I glanced around the auditorium I saw a face peering out from behind one of the pillars; yes, it was him. My stomach churned. Would he be angry or would he heap praise? Something told me it would be the latter. Though I was mistaken – he never said a single word either way. Maybe he was pleased with what he'd seen but just couldn't bring himself to say so.

A familiar face

Like any mother, mine embarrassed me from time to time. The worst incident was when we were walking along Princes Street in

Edinburgh, and all of a sudden she stopped dead in her tracks.

'Look, it's, you know, oh what's his name?' she said, pointing at a couple walking on the other side of the road. She crossed over to them, pulling me behind.

'It's you isn't it? Don't tell me, it's you; we've met before, haven't we?'

The man looked totally surprised and said that no, they'd never met before but it was so nice to meet us.

'Oh, you're American, I knew it, don't tell me, we must have met in America. Or was it in France?'

I was now squirming with embarrassment and decided to put my mother out of her misery. Tugging on her skirt, I whispered:

'Mummy, mummy. It's B...'

'Eunice dear, it's rude to interrupt people's conversations. Now don't tell me, I'll get it in a minute, oh dear...'

'Oh don't worry, what's in a name anyway? I feel we are old friends by now,' the man said sweetly.

I tugged on her skirt yet again and whispered, 'Mum, I am telling you, it's Bi...'

'Eunice, will you please stop? I am trying to talk to this lovely couple.'

They continued chatting for a few more minutes before the man shook my mother's hand, said it was a pleasure to meet her, and they went on their way.

'Now tell me, Eunice dear, did you have any idea who that man was? I hadn't a clue.'

'Mummy, it was Bing Crosby!'

'*Bing Crosby*? Oh good Lord, why didn't you tell me? How embarrassing!'

Rationing

In 1943 times were quite tough; the war was still going on and rationing was in full swing. Luxuries were few and far between and I remember days when my mother and I would walk miles in the freezing cold with an old pram after she'd heard there was a lorry load of coke for sale. The problem was that everyone else had heard the same and by the time we'd passed several prams going the other way, there'd be a few lumps left which we'd have to plead for.

But then there were the times when my Aunt Eunice in America would send us food parcels, most of which were plundered en route, I might add. One day we received some tins of powdered banana from her. There were no cooking instructions so my mother poured one of the tins into a pan, added some water and placed it on the stove; slowly it started to expand and after a short while it erupted like a volcano all over the cooker. Mind you, we didn't dare waste any of it and we lived on banana fritters for weeks on end.

Not that we complained, as any kind of fruit was a real luxury and we always made the best of whatever we had. Of course, sweets and sugar were extremely limited, but I gave my ration to my sister – which resulted in me having a perfect set of teeth without one single cavity or any need to see the dentist, and they remained that way long after the war too.

Towards the end of the war, Father arrived home to tell us we'd be on the move yet again – this time back to Clarkston. I duly enrolled at the Glasgow Academy where I became involved with a school orchestra singing scat. Well, I say singing but it really was just improvised melodies and rhythms.

The move placed further strain on my parents' relationship; so much so, the tense atmosphere in the house severely affected my mother's health. One night when we were getting ready for bed she complained of feeling ill and started shaking like a leaf. I sent out for the doctor and, after examining her, he suspected she'd had some kind of nervous breakdown; the long-term simmering unhappiness between my parents had now taken its toll. She was ill for a long time and, with my father spending a lot of his time away, I missed a whole year of school nursing her.

His uncaring attitude, meanwhile, was blatant. For years, my mother had said that if it wasn't for her family she would have left Father a long time ago. It got to the point where I told her that if she ever used us as an excuse again we would pack up her things and all return to London. When she started to become stronger, yet again she said how she would have left Father if it wasn't for us.

We decided enough was enough. I packed up all our things, told Mother to leave a note for Father, and with that made the long trek back to London. We stayed in a hotel for a while before Mother found us a small cottage in Notting Hill Gate. I never saw my father again.

Though I had my heart set on a career in showbusiness, I knew we needed an income as a priority. As I had now reached school leaving age, I managed to find work as a sales person at Derry and Toms department store on Kensington High Street. It didn't take long for me to develop good customer service skills, which in turn didn't go unnoticed and I was offered the chance to train as a buyer, the person who would attend to a customer's particular needs and help match them up with a product to suit. I told my mother about the promotion opportunity and, realising I was considering a fairly secure and potentially long-term role in retail, she actually suggested I turn the offer down.

She said, 'It will interfere with your ambitions of working in the entertainment industry.'

I ask you, how many parents would say that?

Official secrets

Not too long after our move, a man came to the door one day and told us he had some bad news. He was a government official and informed us our father had died from a massive heart attack while at an airport in Ayr, Scotland.

As I said before, none of us really knew what he did so now seemed an opportune moment to find out. The official said that, because our father was fluent in German and French, and was a lawyer too, he interrogated the captains of captured German U-Boats and warships, and parachutists who'd bailed out from shot-down aircraft. He also taught our agents German and French.

By all accounts he plied prisoners with booze to help extract information from them. Coincidentally we'd noticed, towards the end of our time together, that his drinking was getting heavier. It was put down to difficulties in his marriage, but the truth is, as the drink would be free-flowing, he'd obviously taken advantage himself too. Maybe he wanted to numb the pain of his own existence, who knows? My mother was convinced that he'd actually died of a broken heart but I prefer to think alcohol had taken its toll. Though I suppose one mustn't underestimate the psychological damage caused by the secrecy of his work, or its impact on his family life.

It was a huge shock for us all and quite upsetting, but as we'd not seen him for a year or so I think we all coped pretty well. The man told us that because Father had signed the Official Secrets Act he simply could not discuss any aspect of his work and went on to say that he deserved a posthumous medal, as he'd saved quite a few lives, apparently. It was a real shame, because if we'd known we might have seen him in a different light.

In the happier home environment in London my sister began to make real progress, and was trying to walk again; though often hurting herself in the process, she moved around the room by grabbing onto whatever piece of furniture was to hand. She'd spent so much time in hospital with her leg raised that it actually stunted her growth and she had to wear a heavy metal splint-like contraption to walk, but Mother was convinced her growth could be encouraged to resume and had special boots made. It was so exciting to see her leg lengthening gradually.

In due course Pat began to walk with the aid of two sticks, and then one. Eventually she threw that away and walked unaided. Quite a feat considering the doctors had told my mother not only would she never leave hospital but that she'd never walk again!

On reflection

So there you have it; my childhood, and one I thought pretty unremarkable at the time. However, looking back now, I think it was anything but. The bravery of my dear sister, the love from my brother and the warmth and encouragement from my wonderful mother shaped the rest of my life. Of course I mustn't forget my father; standing up to him from an early age gave me incredible strength and confidence, just what's needed for a career in showbusiness. So perhaps he did me a favour after all?

Chapter Two

My Early Career:
theatre, mediums and the BBC

1946 proved to be a real turning point in my career. Mother, Pat and I had all moved into a large flat in Bayswater, and I left my job at Derry and Toms when I was offered a small part in *Ladies Without* at the Garrick Theatre in London – my very first proper theatre job!

It all started swimmingly, and then one day the producer took me aside and said, 'Your name, Sargaison, it's taking up too much space on the poster. My leading lady is complaining! It's also too cumbersome. Have you ever considered changing it?'

He suggested something shorter and punchier. I wonder what he'd have said to Benedict Cumberbatch? Anyhow, it wasn't something that was at the forefront of my mind, but after discussing it with my mother she suggested I take his advice and came up with the idea of changing it to one of her family names – Berkeley.

'No, no, no,' said the producer. 'It's nearly as long as Sargaison, it needs to be shorter and more memorable.' Back to the drawing board we went, and played around with names for a while before we hit on it: drop the 'Sar', leaving 'Gaison', and change the I to a Y ... GAYSON. That was it! History, as they say, was made.

She's behind you!

In December 1946 I auditioned for, and won the part of, Princess

My Early Career

Luvlee in the Edward Beaumont production of *Aladdin* at the Grand Theatre in Derby. Pantomime is incredibly hard work, with up to three shows a day, but I absolutely loved it. The glare of the footlights, the greasepaint, costumes and audience reaction all combined to cement my absolute desire to be a full-time professional actress.

The pantomime's two weeks were really flying by and the reviews were happily favourable, with *The Stage* even calling me 'vivacious' and 'someone who sings and dances extremely well.' Very flattering indeed, and who was I to argue? Anyhow, one night a rather affluent local lady invited the whole cast back to her house for dinner. Delighted to have an evening away from my rather basic digs, I readily accepted. The stage manager took me, and other cast members, to one side, however, and warned us that not only was our hostess a well-known lesbian with a penchant for pretty young girls, but also quite cuckoo – believing she not only had the power to tell people's fortunes but to contact loved ones calling from the other side. At the time I was still very naïve and had to ask a more mature member of the cast what a 'lesbian' was!

Our hostess was delightful and charming and certainly didn't make any attempt to seduce me, or anyone else for that matter. After dinner she suggested we held a seance in her study. We all positioned ourselves around the huge circular table in the centre of the room and, as instructed, linked hands. I'd never been to anything like it before and had no idea what was going on, but sitting in the dark with just a candle for light really began to freak me out, particularly when our hostess started wailing and asking 'Is anybody there?'

The candle flickered a few times but I sensibly put that down to it being a draughty old house. This went on for a while, and far from freaking me out further I started to feel rather bored with it all. Then, all of a sudden, I felt a pair of hands on my shoulders, pulling me backwards. Yet there was no one behind me!

Madam Arcati was still wailing away and I started to feel detached from all that was going on around me. The hands on my shoulders pulled me to the point where I was fully laid back, looking up at the ceiling. I was conscious but not really, if you can understand where I'm coming from? Nobody said anything to me. Had they not noticed?

I didn't understand what was going on but I could hear Madam Arcati say, 'Now I want you to tell me, there is someone in this room who has a very strong sense of what's going on around us...' She added, 'I want you to tell me, tell me what you feel,' and she went around the table one by one. My fellow cast members started giggling. 'Now come on! I'm being serious! Something is happening in this room.'

She finally came to me and asked what I felt. I tried to speak but started to cough really badly, almost to the point of choking. I sat bolt upright and heard myself saying, 'A man has just come into the room.'

'Who is he?' Madam Arcati asked. 'Could you ask him who he is?' I thought 'She doesn't know who he is? Well, it's her house!'

All the same, I heard myself asking 'Who are you?' He said 'I'm Tracey's uncle,' and with that one of the girls in the cast gasped, 'Oh my God, that voice. But you died in North Africa in the desert, you choked to death...' He said, 'Yes, like I'm choking now.' I began gasping for breath and started coughing again.

'Leave this lady! She's had enough!' Madam exclaimed. With that I found myself sitting at the table, linking hands with everyone just as before. 'Do you believe in the occult?' Madam asked. I didn't know what it meant. 'You have the gift,' she added.

Gift or no gift, I'd had enough and made my excuses, as did everyone else. On the way to our digs I asked who had put their hands on my shoulders and tipped me backwards, but my cast mates all looked at me, puzzled. They said I hadn't moved from the table, and certainly not backwards in my chair.

I didn't question them further, nor did I accept any more dinner invitations!

However, that night at my digs I was woken by a loud crash. When I turned the light on, I saw my large suitcase had fallen off the top of the wardrobe. I put it back, switched the light off and went back to sleep. Not long afterwards it happened again ... and then a third time. I mentioned it next morning at breakfast and a fellow cast member said he thought it might have been a mischievous spirit – or, as we know them better, a poltergeist – which had latched on to me at the seance. He recommended I just tell it to 'Leave me alone.'

The next night, and the night after, it happened again. No matter how nicely or sharply I said 'Leave me alone,' it would not – that is, until I really yelled. Miraculously it all stopped just as quickly as it had started. However, it showed me I was vulnerable to such happenings, though thankfully my 200-year-old cottage today only has friendly spirits!

Richmond Theatre

Back in London, and between jobs as we say in the profession, I answered an advertisement for an assistant stage manager position at Richmond Theatre repertory company.

The interview went very well and I started work with duties including ensuring everyone was where they were supposed to be, and on time; ensuring the required props were on hand, and prompting the actors whenever they forgot their cues or lines; things like that. As I'd only a little acting experience at this point, I thought it was not only a great way to get the best seat in the house but, as the ASM had to be 'on the book', I could learn the plays and know every line like the back of my hand too.

My first audition at the rep was for *Little Women*, which was terrific fun and a great experience. I then appeared in quite a few shows, one of which was *The Barretts of Wimpole Street*, in which

I played Vicky. After a week or two in Richmond we went on a huge nationwide tour, and that really gave me a strong touring identity. And the money was rather good too, so after I'd paid for my digs I was able to send some home to my mother.

Many of the lead roles in Richmond shows were cast with stars of West End productions, when they were either coming in or going out of town, as 'guests' of the theatre. One such production was *Born Yesterday* and its star was the great American actor Hartley Power, who arrived following a hugely successful London run. His leading lady, Yolande Donlan (who later became Mrs Val Guest), had to return to the USA, so Richmond proposed our own leading lady, who was rather grand and frightfully English with a voice to match. Her role, though, required a Bronx accent, which, try as she might, she just could not master.

At the first rehearsal Hartley Power was furious and thought her casting was some kind of joke. 'You've got me here and you don't have a leading lady who can do a New York accent? You have to be kidding me! Are there any actresses here who can manage it?' he boomed.

Everyone in the company looked quite sheepish, and no one dared step forward just in case their attempt wasn't up to scratch and they too incurred his wrath. He looked over at me and asked if I was an actress. As I opened my mouth to reply, he added, 'Can you do a Brooklyn accent?'

I did have a fairly good ear, and being a keen cinemagoer I had heard all sorts of American accents. I took a deep breath and said 'Er, well, of course I can sir' in my best New York style.

'My God, that's perfect! Get yourself up here!'

Without time to protest I was thrust forward and handed a script. His (now) ex-leading lady was, understandably, very upset. Never mind having Hartley Power question her abilities as an actress but upstaging her with a lowly assistant stage manager … that was simply the final straw. She made it known that she'd never been so insulted in all her life and promptly resigned from the company, never to be seen again!

Being 'on the book' I knew the play pretty well already, which was a relief as we opened in a few days, but then it really hit me. I was going to be performing with one of the American greats and if I messed up it may be my last appearance on any stage.

My hair at the time was very long, as was the fashion with most teenagers, and Hartley Power said, 'You know, you don't look dumb enough to play this girl in the script. Could you get a blonde rinse just to make you look a bit stoopid?'

As we were opening that very night the director said, 'I can't spare you, we're lighting and rehearsing; there just isn't time to go to the hairdresser now.'

'Can't you just send out for something?' Power asked.

So some sort of dye arrived at the theatre and was put on my hair. We carried on lighting and rehearsing with my hair wrapped in a towel. An hour later the towel was removed and the dresser screamed 'Aaaaaaaaaaaaaaaaaaaah!'

I looked in a mirror. My hair had turned green; the dye had been left on for too long!

The audience was beginning to arrive and in desperation one of the dressers pulled out a pot of gold dust, and with a bit of hair tonic rubbed it all over my head. We opened and I delivered my lines with my head held fairly rigid so as the gold dust – which was like a bizarre sort of talcum powder – wouldn't drop out. By the end of the play it too was going green. Mercifully, from the audience it looked reasonably OK – but do you think I could get it out afterwards?

Thankfully the reviews were good, and I completed the run unscathed, aside from a few sessions in the hairdresser's chair. I really must thank not only Hartley Power but his 'frightfully, frightfully' English former leading lady for giving me my first big break.

Mrs 10 %

With a few credits under my belt, I felt it was time to get myself
an agent and pursue yet more exciting opportunities. I was
introduced to Monti Macky by a friend, and she was keen to
represent me. Monti immediately got me a small part (so small I
went uncredited) in a film called *Meet Me At Dawn*; the producer
was Marcel Hellman, a Romanian who came over to the UK and
partnered with Douglas Fairbanks Jr, whom I ended up working for
a decade later.

I remember being on set at Denham Studios for the first
time. The bustle, the noise, the smell of paint and fresh timber;
it was all quite magical. The cast was a Who's Who: Stanley
Holloway, Wilfrid Hyde-White, Margaret Rutherford, Hazel
Court, Katie Johnson (who later won hearts as Mrs Wilberforce
in *The Ladykillers*) and in similar uncredited roles to mine were
Charles Hawtrey, Guy Rolfe and Shelagh Fraser. American director
Thornton Freeland stood behind the camera and explained
where my marks were, how I had to treat the camera – as though
it wasn't there – and generally how to act for the screen rather
than the theatre. There was no need to project my voice, nor to
accentuate facial expressions.

Watching the all-star cast at work was a great learning
experience, and even if I didn't get much screen time myself, at
least I'd been to a film studio, I thought.

My agent, Monti, announced she was joining the Al Parker
agency and was taking me with her. Our new working relationship
kicked off nicely when Monti secured me a singing spot on
Designed for Women, the BBC's first magazine style programme
devoted, not surprisingly, to women. It was to be my television
debut. In those days there was no video recording equipment;
everything was transmitted live from the BBC's studios in
Alexandra Palace, mistakes and all.

My Early Career

It was a fairly stressful experience for everyone; the budgets were on a shoestring and everything was crammed into two small studios using equipment which could, without warning, break down at any moment.

I dread to think how I came across, as I was a bag of nerves, but I must have made a favourable impression because in late 1947 my agent wrote to the BBC asking if there were any future upcoming productions which I was suitable for (it's hard to believe that in those days you could do that) and I received a reply enquiring if I was free on 12 December to test for a part in their new flagship programme aimed at teenagers – *The Teen-Age Show*.

I recently unearthed my old audition card at the BBC archive, which read: 'Has a very good voice and is very appealing in a provocative way. Should prove very useful all round television.'

I'm guessing they liked me as not only was I booked for the *The Teen-Age Show* in January 1948 but also for several other BBC shows such as *Between Ourselves*, *Spring Revue*, *Consider Your Verdict*, *Lady Luck* and *Halesapoppin*. The last of these was a one-off special for popular comedian Sonnie Hale and also featured Doris Hare, who later found fame as Mum in *On the Buses*.

Also during this period, I appeared in Louis D'Alton's *They Got What They Wanted* for Dublin's Abbey Theatre Players. They'd performed the play at the Embassy Theatre in Swiss Cottage and earned rave reviews. It was all set to transfer to the Phoenix Theatre in the West End, but the management didn't particularly like the girl playing the lead and let it be known they were looking for someone else.

Among the cast were Charles Fitzsimons and his brother, who were the siblings of film star Maureen O'Hara. Now Charlie, who was one of the company's leading players in Dublin, had seen me in a couple of things and said, 'You have an Irish background!' (My father was half-Irish.) He asked to hear my Irish accent and thought it was good; well, he said I 'wasn't far wrong' and then trained me to do it properly. So I auditioned for the role and got it. We opened at the Phoenix but the play was only programmed to run a few months so it was a relatively short-lived engagement. Meanwhile, Charlie became my first proper boyfriend, and through him I became very friendly with Maureen O'Hara.

In demand

Getting an agent like Monti was a really positive move as more film work soon came along in the guise of *It Happened in Soho*, a drama in which I played a character called Julie, a very small part. But then, in my next film, *My Brother Jonathan*, I got a slightly bigger role and a chance to work with James Robertson Justice, Michael Denison and Dulcie Gray. Michael and Dulcie became very close friends, and the sage advice they gave me was absolutely invaluable.

Another film part in *Melody in the Dark* was swiftly followed by *The Huggetts Abroad*, which starred some really heavyweight acting talent of the day, including Jack Warner, Dinah Sheridan, her then husband Jimmy Hanley, and a 17-year-old Petula Clark.

With hardly time to blink I was back in the theatre with a musical called *Goodnight Vienna*, during which time the BBC came calling to enrol me in yet more nerve-wracking live television, playing Emily Strachan in *Pink String and Sealing Wax*. Thankfully I managed to get through it without any major mishaps; well, apart from the odd door handle coming off in my hand or the scenery occasionally wobbling. In those days you learned to think on your feet and just get on with it – a good job, really, as my next assignment, *The Director*, really tested my patience.

Before I get into that, talking about live television reminds me of a TV production of *The Duchess of Malfi* which I appeared in with that Grande Dame of theatre, Irene Worth. I played one of her handmaidens and had to be at the Duchess's bedside for her death scene, as any good handmaiden would. I must stress this really was a big climax, and a very important scene.

My Early Career

Irene gave a rip-roaring performance throughout the whole show and then died in the most convincing and beautiful way. After about 30 seconds, she pulled herself up in the bed and said, rather loudly, 'Thank God that's over,' totally unaware that we were still very much live on TV.

I said from the side of my mouth, 'You've got to die again.'

She went from dead to live to dead again in the most dramatic fashion until the gallery finally announced that we were off the air. Irene apparently hadn't done live TV before, and thought the whole experience was 'a great learning curve'. I'm not sure the gallery would have shared her opinion!

I digress. Back to October 1949 when I was booked to play Katie in the BBC television production of *The Director*. It was produced and directed by Kevin Sheldon, whom I'd worked with before on *Pink String and Sealing Wax*. A very well-known American actor had been cast as the Director, and at every opportunity he let it be known what a coup it was for us to have him star in a little old British television show. Such was his own high opinion of his talents he didn't feel it necessary to turn up for rehearsals; little did he know that this was one of the BBC's most ambitious live projects to date ... nor what could possibly go wrong!

One of my scenes involved rushing into the local pub and asking the Director, in my best Irish accent of course, if he had 'seen me da?'

Simple, or so you may think.

I ran up to the Director and delivered my line only to be met with a look of absolute terror. I repeated the line again and he just stood there staring at me, totally blank. The guys in the gallery were tearing their hair out wondering what the hell was going on; time was ticking, they needed to move to the next set-up, and his reply to my line was imperative. As I'd done a few of these live broadcasts before I realised you'd sometimes have to improvise a little, and as this guy hadn't a clue what was going on I proceeded to ask the entire pub if they'd 'seen me da' to take the focus off our star. Luckily one of the extras had been to the rehearsals that afternoon and had remembered the next line,

'Yeah, I've seen your da. Is he the one with the red flannel necktie and flat cap?' he said.

'Yeah, that's me da, did ya see where he was going?' I asked.

'Yeah, I think he was going up to Bunty's place to meet his brother … and then on to meet … er …'

'Trevor! Was he going to meet Trevor, do ya know?' I added.

'Yeah that's it, he was going to meet Trevor,' he said. And with that I rushed out of the door and onto the next scene.

How we ever got through the 78 set-ups I will never know, but did I ever thank that extra when we were off air for saving the scene. He said he'd worked on a few live productions where actors had dried (as we say in the business). It's just a shame he wasn't paid anything extra for saving the whole show.

I rounded off 1949 with another theatre gig in the shape of Reginald Long's *The Wife Jumped Over the Moon*, followed by another appearance on *Designed for Women* and finally the BBC's live production of *Dick Whittington* for Christmas, in which I played 'Girl'.

The ensuing few years were fairly hectic but in all honesty I just loved working and certainly learned never to turn any kind of work down, as you'd always learn something new with every job.

Chapter Three

Love and Marriage

M y first encounter with Hammer Films was in 1950, a fair few years before they became synonymous with the horror genre. *To Have and To Hold* was directed by Godfrey Grayson and shot at Hammer's studio at Gilston Park – a former country club – in Hertfordshire, shortly before they moved to their studios in Bray, Berkshire.

In the story a man is crippled after a horse-riding accident and, realising he is coming to the end of his life, spends the rest of his days trying to take care of his family and encouraging his wife to find another man. It was just another typical British melodrama.

The opening credits announced 'Introducing Eunice Gayson', suggesting Hammer had somehow discovered me. Granted I hadn't made that many excursions onto the silver screen but, come on, it was hardly a discovery; that's PR for you!

I played an aspiring singer, Peggy, and although the film wasn't anything too exciting it did reasonably well at the box-office and a song was specially written for me. It was such an odd feeling, walking down Charing Cross Road afterwards, glancing in shop windows and seeing 'Eunice Gayson sings *To Have and To Hold*' on sheet music and records! It did in fact open up many other musical avenues for me, which I shall write more about later.

It was then back to the BBC for more of their live dramas including: *Alice, Here Come the Boys, Treasures in Heaven,* and *Mother of Men* with Barbara Mullen, who was a huge Irish star at the time. This was the second time I used my rather convincing Irish brogue, and I was ever grateful for my good ear for accents.

Diana

Amid all the live TV drama I managed to squeeze in some more film appearances, one being *Dance Hall*, an Ealing Studios production directed by Charles Crichton. I remember this film most fondly for the cast: Donald Houston, Petula Clark, Kay Kendall, Dandy Nicholls and a certain Miss Diana Fluck, who was more famously known as Diana Dors. In fact, it was during this film that we cemented a life-long friendship.

Di was a huge personality; she was larger than life, and boy did she love life. We met regularly for lunch and dinners, stayed with each other abroad and at home, and were always there to support one another. The thing about Diana which people didn't realise was that she was essentially a very down-to-earth girl. Once the glamorous dresses and make-up came off she loved nothing better than to slip into casual clothes and lead a normal family life. The extrovert actress who 'put it on' for the public was very different to the Di I knew – a mother who deeply loved her boys and a great, great friend to many people. When her final illness took her in 1984 a big light went out in my life.

I, like many others, must admit to not always approving of Di's choice in men. She had a very good eye for scripts and always knew where she wanted to be in her life and career, and would get there. But the men in her life were, on the whole, bad for her.

The first time I stayed with Di in California she was doing cabaret in Las Vegas in an attempt to break into the American market, and that's a hard nut to crack, believe me. Everyone was saying she'd never do it, but Di was a huge hit and was absolutely terrific! She started doing all sorts of TV appearances and suddenly became THE person in Hollywood to invite to a party.

Love and Marriage

Anyway, I was out in Las Vegas visiting Di and hopped in to a lift in one of the hotels – only for a thuggish-looking guy to get in beside me.

'Hey, I believe you're a friend of Diana Dors?' he said.

'Who are you?' I asked.

'Never mind who I am, I wanna meet your friend Diana Dors.'

I thought, 'My God, she needs this guy like a hole in the head.' So I said, 'Yes, sure, do you have a card?'

He handed me one and said, 'I'm sure she'd be delighted to meet up with me, everybody knows me.'

Well, I didn't! So I asked one of the hotel staff who he was. 'Are you kidding me? You don't know who that guy is? He's Mafia.'

There was no way I was going to tell Diana about the incident in the lift, as she'd have wanted to meet him for sure. She was like that! Though she attracted a lot of the wrong guys, there were some nice ones who wanted to meet Di too, some quite delightful in fact. George Hamilton was one, I remember; when I met him in LA and happened to say I was staying with Di, he immediately said, 'I'd love to meet Diana Dors!'

Di had the most fabulous figure; I mean, no kidding, she looked amazing. Who wouldn't want to meet her? She knew it too, and took great care of herself. She would never kneel, for instance, because, she said earnestly, 'It might dent my knees and they might not come back.' I always knew she was a good actress, and a very underrated one; excepting one or two performances, she was sadly never given the credit she really deserved.

She always tried to fix me up with guys too, but her recommendations were pretty poor. The people she picked were usually married for a start, though that never worried her; she could be a very naughty girl like that. Cupid antics aside, I always enjoyed her company and I think she enjoyed mine. She used to say to me when I was talking about somebody in her life whom I didn't think was good for her, 'Here endeth the lesson.' And I said,

'No, it isn't ending yet, I've got more to say...' But she didn't take one bit of notice.

In later life, I was happy she married Alan Lake because she absolutely adored him and he worshipped the ground she walked on. Each of them had had very chequered love lives but had seemingly found their soul mate at last. He often said to her, 'I hope to God I go first as I couldn't live without you.' Tragically, after Di's death, Alan committed suicide – he really couldn't live without her.

Kay

Another great friend of mine who was also taken too early was the beautiful Kay Kendall. Kay met and fell head over heels in love with Rex Harrison after working with him on *The Constant Husband* in 1955, though I don't know why as he was disliked by virtually everyone in the business. And he was still married to Lilli Palmer.

When Rex was in *My Fair Lady*, the original stage production with Julie Andrews, he became a sensation. It transferred to Broadway in 1956 and I went to see it. Now, I didn't know Julie Andrews that well, but when I popped backstage after the performance to say how much I enjoyed it, she was very courteous and said she always 'loved seeing someone from back home.' Rex, on the other hand, just grunted.

Slow dissolve to a couple of days later ... Kay and I were having lunch together at Sardi's and we were laughing away over coffee when, suddenly, she asked 'What time is it?' It was about 3.30 pm or something like that. 'Oh my God, I've got to get to the theatre … Stay here, I'll be back.'

There is a song in the show called 'I've Grown Accustomed to Her Face', which Rex hated with a passion. In fact, he said 'It's got to go' to the management, but they said 'No, no, it's one of the big hits in the show!' Rex made such a fuss about it, as he did most things, so the management asked what the problem was. He said, 'I don't feel like that when I look at Julie Andrews. I don't like her.'

I mean, what a bitchy remark!

Anyhow, they said 'You're an actor, act it.' Then of course there was a stand-off. 'Well, if it doesn't go, I've got to leave the show,' he whined. He thought for a moment, perhaps worried they might fire him, and added 'But if Kay was standing at the side of the stage I could sing the song, as I love *her* face.' So forever after, Kay had to go to every performance while he sang that number.

Anyway, 20 minutes later she came rushing back. 'I'm so sorry,' she said. 'I have to plan my day round it.'

Kay was always so much fun and such a warm character, unlike Rex. That said, he loved nothing more than to just sit and look at her, as though he was bathing in her beauty. I will say, though, that when he discovered Kay had myeloid leukaemia, he and Lilli Palmer agreed to divorce in order for him to marry Kay and care for her. I remember Lilli Palmer saying she was not upset at the divorce because *she* had a lover too! The pair supposedly planned to remarry after Kay's death, but Lilli married her boyfriend Carlos Thompson instead.

Kay meanwhile was never told of her illness and ended up believing she just had an iron deficiency. She died in September 1959.

Footlights

1951 was very much a transitional year for me. I'd spent the last couple of years happily hopping from live BBC television dramas to the odd film, but I felt it was time for a fresh challenge. I'd always loved theatre and the urge to slap on the greasepaint and tread the boards again was overwhelming.

As luck would have it I decided to visit one of my favourite little theatres, The New Lindsey in Notting Hill Gate, to see a matinée and on arriving saw a poster for an upcoming production, *The*

Lonely Heart. At the very moment it caught my eye a woman walked past and said, 'Hello, I'm Judith Warden. Are you here for the audition?' she asked.

'What audition?' I enquired.

'We're interviewing for parts in my play, *The Lonely Heart* ... You look like an actress so thought I would just ask.'

I explained that I was indeed an actress, although I'd just arrived early for the matinée performance. Not one to waste an opportunity, I cheekily asked if I could audition anyway. My bravado paid off; she said she had no objection if I went through there and then.

Of course, I had nothing prepared but managed to rustle something up from the memory bank. Don't ask me what it was as I can't remember, but whatever it was that I performed off the top of my head landed me the lead role of Lindsay Thatcher. How about that?

The Lonely Heart was quite a daring play for its time, tackling the subject of lesbianism. In her early life my character was encouraged by her mother to be very boyish, both in attitude and clothes, as her mother had hoped for a son. Now grown up, Lindsay shared a flat with Suzanne (described in the script as a 'very feminine' girl), whom Lindsay was continually rude and blasé towards, meanwhile drinking beer, wearing trousers and wearing her hair pushed back – all signs, evidently, of perceived 1950s' masculinity.

As the play progressed it became obvious that this was actually a story about how Lindsay was concealing a passionate love for her flatmate Suzanne, a passion so powerful she (unsuccessfully) tried to end her life when the object of her desire announced she was getting married and moving to New York. Turning to her cold-hearted mother for support, Lindsay was dismissively told to 'Pull yourself together,' but instead decided to take a friendly doctor's advice and visit a psychiatrist. There, she pulled off her tie, shook out her long attractive hair, looked into the mirror and was told to have confidence in herself, and to be true to her own feelings. It was nothing to be ashamed of.

It sounds a little clichéd now but you have to remember that this was the 1950s. While these days no one would blink an eye, a relationship between two women back then, though not illegal, suffered severe prejudice and discrimination. But this play was all about self-discovery and in that respect was way ahead of its time; in fact, I received a few letters from women thanking me for my performance and for showing one should always be true to one's self.

The Lonely Heart received mixed reviews, which was not really surprising given its theme, but it was a production I was immensely proud to be involved with – and one which certainly helped take my career in a direction away from 'safe' television stories.

I was next invited to play the part of Vicky Hobson in a revival of Harold Brighouse's Lancashire comedy *Hobson's Choice*; rather appropriately, we were to perform twice-nightly during the summer at the Grand Theatre in Blackpool, in the very heart of Lancashire. It was hard work doing two shows a night, but I just loved being back on stage and hearing the reaction from the audience to this lovely comedy. That's something I missed in TV and films, and it gave me a huge surge of excitement and energy.

The cast included the late, great Wilfred Pickles, who had famously spent many years as the host of the BBC radio show *Have a Go*, and his wife Mabel. Mabel was an intensely jealous woman who scowled at any actress who so much as spoke to Wilfred, and as a further measure of protection she'd always escort him from his dressing room to the stage and back again. Wilfred was hardly what you'd call a looker, so no one really understood why she was so jealous. But then again, never judge a book by its cover.

With two good stage plays under my belt I happened to mention to a friend of mine, who worked in the music department at the BBC, that despite all my training as a singer I hadn't really done much of it on screen. And I'd so enjoyed singing in *To Have and To Hold*.

He said, 'Look, I've got an operetta called *La Belle Helene* coming up...'

I asked to be considered, and happily was eventually cast. It gave me an entrée into musical shows, and I did quite a lot of them in quick succession for the Beeb with the Eric Robinson Orchestra – *Music for You* and *The David Hughes Show*. That one conversation opened up the musical side of my life, standing me in good stead for *The Sound of Music*, of which more a little later.

Topical

As you've read, I've always been the type of person who likes to challenge myself and take risks with my career. So after many years of playing straight (with the odd bit of lesbianism) theatre I decided to push the envelope a little more and move into another style of performance – revue. The popular genre had been around in theatres for years and was essentially based around songs and sketches satirising whatever was in the news.

My involvement came about in the autumn of 1951 when producer/director Michael Mills (who later became Head of Light Entertainment at the BBC and married fellow Bond girl Valerie Leon) started putting together a Christmas show. He asked if I would be his leading lady; apparently he thought I was a very versatile actress, as he'd seen through my various BBC plays, which was deemed 'essential' for this kind of production.

I asked him if he had a venue in mind for the show. He didn't so I suggested the New Lindsey Theatre in Notting Hill. Opening on Boxing Day 1951, *Ring in the New* also starred Cardew Robinson, Ian Ainsley, Gail Kendall, Louie Ramsay, Pat MacLauchlan, Robert Arden and Bruce Gordon, many of whom went on to become household names.

Love and Marriage

It was a real 'seat of the pants' experience, as with the news constantly changing so were our scripts, with writers frantically re-writing dialogue and songs minutes before we went on stage. You certainly had to be on the ball I can tell you, and thankfully my days of repertory had instilled in me a strong 'just get on with it' attitude.

One of the songs in the show, 'For You And Me', turned out to have been written by a 15-year-old drama student from Camberley, Surrey, named Janet Edwardes. Janet had been cast in a little film about the girl guides called *Journey for Vicky*, and to fill in time between takes she started tinkering on the piano. The next thing she knew, someone on set heard the melody and thought it would make a good song. The press officer of the Guides Association, Molly Podger, wrote some lyrics and it was used in the film. Subsequently someone thought it should be in our Christmas revue.

Why am I telling you all this? Well, roll forward six decades to 2012 and the opening of the 'Bond in Motion' exhibition in Beaulieu. I was there to cut the ribbon, as was Jenny Hanley, who in turn brought her friend Janet with her. Yes! The very same Janet Edwardes (now Benney).

Fortunately, the trade papers raved about my performance, so much so that the leading American trade, *Billboard*, sent along their London correspondent Leigh Vance to interview me. 'What does this limey girl have that's so special?' they wanted to know. To say the interview went well would be an understatement – we got on like a house on fire! Leigh invited me to dinner, we became a couple, and the rest, as they say, is history.

Six months after our first meeting Leigh asked me to marry him and I accepted. It was all a bit of a whirlwind, to be honest, and, as we both had current work commitments, we decided to set the date for about a year later.

My starring in *Ring in the New* caught the attention of Peter Myers and Alex Grahame, two of the wittiest revue writers of the period who, along with screenwriter and composer Ronald Cass, had established the Irving Theatre in London's Leicester Square. In March 1952, I was cast, along with Barbara Pierce, Betty Marsden, Michael Medwin and a then little known American actor named Larry Hagman, in their new production, appropriately entitled *The Irving Revue*. It was the usual mix of songs and sketches you associated with the genre, and included Larry and Barbara debunking American teenagers in 'Bobby Sox Ballad', and myself, Barbara and Pamela Manson skitting the Brontë sisters.

It certainly wasn't a very glamorous setting. The Irving was promoted as the West End's smallest theatre, and that was true back stage, too, with 14 people and only one tiny dressing room; things certainly became, shall we say, rather intimate! However, there was little time for any embarrassment as we'd often only have 30 seconds to change (much to the surprise of Larry, who I think was used to more traditional theatre). One minute you'd be throwing talcum powder in your hair to play a 90-year-old, the next you'd be glamming up to portray Marilyn Monroe.

I certainly learned 'anything is possible' from my time in revue. It was a great training ground and offered wonderful opportunities to newcomers.

Gooning around

I'm sure a large majority of actors will tell you that the old adage 'it's not what you know it's who you know' rings true. If you work with a director or producer and do your job properly, without causing any kind of fuss, they will use you again and again. In June 1952 I was cast in a one-off BBC drama entitled *Nine Til Six*, and a few days afterwards my agent called to say Michael Mills from the BBC had been in touch again. Now, you remember I'd worked with Michael on *Ring in the New* at the New Lindsey Theatre? Well, he was now looking for actors for a pilot TV show called *Goonreel*, which would parody, as the title suggests, the newsreels of the time. It was to star the BBC's biggest names – The Goons.

Now, for those of you who weren't born in the Dark Ages, The Goons were Peter Sellers, Spike Milligan, Michael Bentine and Harry Secombe; their surreal brand of comedy was a huge hit on the radio, with millions tuning in each week. Some bright spark at the BBC then decided, quite rightly, it would be a good idea to transfer their unique antics to the small screen. Without any hesitation whatsoever I said 'Yes.' The chance to work with Britain's foremost comedians was a real no-brainer.

Rehearsals were an absolute blast as The Goons were terrible pranksters. I'd be expecting the next line from Peter Sellers in front of me, and Michael Bentine would deliver it from behind; it really kept me on my toes. I liked them all immensely and, although I didn't really get to know them that well on a personal level, I got the feeling they were pretty much the same off screen as they were on.

The top brass at BBC Television were a bit more straight-laced than those in radio, it seemed, and frowned at The Goons' 'tomfoolery'. They often dispatched accountants down to the set to keep an eye on things. Not only were The Goons considered to be wasting precious studio time with their practical jokes, constant re-writes and diversions from the script, but the sets themselves had cost a fortune to build and part of the gag was that they'd now all fall down. You see, The Goons had pretty much a free creative rein in radio, and this irked the BBC bean-counters, who were used to seeing the final script and allocating a final budget in advance. You'd often see these anxious 'suits' standing around, chewing their fingernails wondering how much more money was being spent and on what; in fact, it's a wonder they had any nails left.

The practical jokes weren't limited to the studio either; one night, after rehearsals, Michael Bentine offered me a lift home, which I thought was most kind. There's nothing nicer than being taken to your front door after a hard day, rather than braving the tube, so imagine my horror when we walked into the car park and he led me to his bicycle!

Goonreel was transmitted on 2 July 1952 in front of a live studio audience. A huge amount of time and money had been invested in the 45-minute show and thankfully it paid off. The audience screamed the place down and absolutely loved it.

Afterwards everyone agreed we'd struck comedy gold and were positive the BBC would commission a full series. Alas, it wasn't to be. Perhaps this was one of the first instances of the accountants flexing their muscles at the BBC? They'd argued this was one of the most expensive TV shows they'd ever made, and a series would be economically out of the question. We were all stunned but they said their decision was final.

Cigarettes and alcohol

Shortly after *Goonreel*, I was cast as Louka in the BBC's production of George Bernard Shaw's *Arms and the Man*. This was one of Shaw's shorter full-length plays and was a light comedy set during the Serbo-Bulgarian War. It was to be transmitted live from the BBC's Lime Grove Studios in Shepherd's Bush (formerly Gainsborough Film Studios) as part of the *Sunday Night Theatre* series, and was directed by Tatiana Lieven, for whom I'd worked in *Nine Til Six* back in June.

I knew playing Louka would be a challenge; the character had a penchant for smoking and drinking quite heavily and I'd never touched a cigarette in my life. Imagine my horror when I arrived on the first day of rehearsals and was handed a glass of whisky (well, whisky-coloured water) and a packet of cigarettes and was expected to smoke, drink and talk all at the same time! I explained to Tatiana that I'd never smoked and asked if the script could be changed to accommodate this? She looked down her nose at me and said, 'Of course not, Eunice dear, one simply does not change Shaw'.

Love and Marriage

Luckily, I wasn't required on set for a while and figured I could spend the time learning to smoke a cigarette. It was the early 1950s and it was fashionable to smoke; in fact, everybody was doing it. So how hard could it be?

I lit my first cigarette and immediately felt sick to my stomach as the acrid grey smoke drifted up my nostrils. I really didn't know how the hell I was going to get through rehearsals, never mind a live television performance. I cautiously took my first drag and started to cough. My face went bright red and my eyes bulged as I exhaled this hideous substance that was actually burning my throat and lungs.

After a while, and a few coughing fits later, it seemed to get a little easier, so I felt confident enough to get through rehearsals at least. I was duly called down for the first set-up; Tatiana signalled from the gallery and I delivered my line before confidently taking a drag of the cigarette ... I then started to cough and, though I tried to deliver the next line, it was just no good, I had to stop. A voice from the gallery boomed, 'Come on, Eunice dear, I can't hear a word you're saying, speak up.'

Fast forward to 27 July 1952 and Lime Grove was absolutely buzzing as we prepared for the live transmission. I arrived on set and was handed my usual props of a glass of fake whisky and a packet of cigarettes. Hang on! I knew very little about smoking but I did know that Sobranie cigarettes, which I'd been given, were one of the strongest in the world. I'd been practicing with a much milder brand, so rushed over to Tatiana in a mild panic and explained my predicament.

'Eunice dear, the play is set in Bulgaria and these are Russian cigarettes. You're an actress, get on with it,' she said as the red transmission light came on.

As soon as I took a drag I felt the back of my throat burn. We were live at this point and I thought 'To hell with Shaw', almost throwing in a line of my own: 'I really must give up this filthy habit.' But, of course, one never changes Shaw.

Thinking on my feet I picked up the 'whisky', hoping a swig would calm the sensation. As I tipped the glass I saw a huge wasp in it. 'Oh God,' I thought, 'how can things possibly get any worse?' But I had no choice and swallowed some of the water. Thankfully, by the time the glass touched my lips the wasp had drowned and wasn't in a stinging mood, so I managed to get through the rest of the show without any major hiccups. I breathed such a huge of sigh of relief when the red transmission light went off.

Before Tatiana had chance to castigate me I told her what had happened and she thanked me for being a true professional. Talk about suffering for your art!

More Gooning around

I'd obviously made an impression on The Goons as I was invited to be part of their next project, a feature film entitled *Down Among the Z Men*. The producer was Edwin J Fancey, who was quite well known for making low-budget B-movies. Well, to say the budget was low on this film would be an understatement!

They'd allotted a two-week shooting schedule and I was later told by Michael Bentine that money was so tight the director, Maclean Rogers, told everyone up front that he would only allow one take of each scene unless something truly disastrous occurred. I'm not sure what 'disastrous' meant exactly, as if you listen carefully to the finished film you can hear off-camera stagehands laughing out loud at times.

The plot involved some shifty crooks trying to fiddle an honest yet gullible buffoon. It was quite a successful formula and went on to become the basis for virtually every *Goon Show* episode on radio thereafter. However, the madcap humour The Goons were famous for on radio wasn't really evident, despite the film featuring a few established radio characters.

I believe the chaos and fun of the radio show was due primarily to Spike Milligan's writing; it was as zany as he was. The film's writing chores were offered to Jimmy Grafton (who worked on *Goonreel*) and Francis Charles, neither of whom succeeded in replicating the magic.

The film wasn't much of a success in UK cinemas and, as the foursome were unheard of Stateside, there was no theatrical release in America at all. The Goons never attempted another movie together; however, once Peter Sellers became a big star, 16mm pirate copies of *Z Men* started appearing on the market under the moniker *The Goon Show Movie*.

Success or not, I was more than happy to spend a little more time with the chaps. Soon after the film Michael Bentine quit the radio series, citing clashes with Spike, and the show continued with the three remaining actors until 1960. Prince Charles named it his favourite show while growing up, which is no bad accolade to have!

Robbing the rich

I was really on a roll when my agent called and told me I'd been short-listed for a part in the film *Miss Robin Hood*. It was for a company called Group 3 Productions who owned and ran the three-stage Southall Studios in West London. It sounded like great fun and the cream of British comedy talent of the time were lined up to star: as well as the wonderful Margaret Rutherford, there were Dora Bryan, James Robertson Justice, Ian Carmichael, Kenneth Connor, Peter Jones, Sid James, Reg Varney and Michael Medwin.

The premise of the story involved a writer, Henry Wrigley (played by Richard Hearne, better known as Mr Pastry on TV – and a huge star as a result), who created a strip cartoon entitled 'Miss Robin Hood' for a popular children's comic, 'The Teenager'. She was described as being a latterday version of the legendary hero and, with the aid of some teenage girls, robbed the rich to give to the poor.

I was up for the role of Pam, a fresh young girl with a great sense of humour. Perfect for me, or so I thought.

While I was waiting to be called in to meet the director, the door opened and in walked this terrific-looking young girl in a rather revealing top and a short tight skirt, below which were the most gorgeous legs imaginable. I was envious to say the least! She looked me up and down and asked if I was there for the audition, in a manner that seemed to say 'You won't get it looking like that.' I thought there and then I should just get up and go home; how on earth could I compete with her?

I was duly called and read a scene with Margaret Rutherford, which was a great privilege in itself, but my heart was heavy knowing that the stunning girl waiting outside would walk in after me, blow them all away and get the gig.

Miss Rutherford remarked that I was 'sweet', which is not really what I wanted to hear. I wanted to hear that I was 'perfect' or 'just the type we're looking for'. I left feeling quite deflated.

On arriving home my mother asked how it all went. I told her not so good.

Little did I know that the director, John Guillermin (who later went on to make terrific films like *The Blue Max* and *Death on the Nile*), had called while I was on the way home, and told my mother that both he and Miss Rutherford were really impressed and I was 'just the type of girl' they were looking for. They felt the other girl was 'far too provocative' for the part. I had a feeling of total elation, but part of me was a little upset that they saw me as a plain Jane instead of a sultry sex bomb. Now I know you're going to ask about the other girl. Well, I believe her name was Joan Collins. Whatever happened to her?

Making an impression

Cicely Courtneidge – later to become Dame Cicely – had seen me in *The Irving Revue* and offered me the second lead in a show she was going to star in at the Casino Theatre. It was called *Over the Moon* and was directed by her husband Jack Hulbert, whom I'd previously worked with on the BBC drama *Here Come the Boys* in 1953.

Cicely and Jack had worked together for over 30 years, both on stage and in film, primarily in comedies and musicals, and were considered the doyens of the West End. Now they were moving into the very popular revue format and wanted little old me to join them in poking fun at the celebrities and news stories of the day.

Before my pen touched the contract I informed the management that 1 July 1953 had been fixed as my wedding date, and asked for a week's leave of absence to be incorporated.

'Sure,' they said, 'no problem at all.' So I signed on the dotted line.

On the first day of rehearsals I arrived particularly early; as you know, I had a reputation of always being on time and still to this day cannot bear being late for an appointment. Some of the cast started arriving but Cicely, or 'Cis' as we liked to call her, wasn't due for another 15 minutes or so. To keep everyone amused and to break the ice a little, I went into a number she was noted for – 'Vitality', from the Ivor Novello musical *Gay's the Word*. The whole cast fell about with laughter but, when I finished, far from hearing applause, an eerie silence fell over the room along with some very worried looks. One cast member mouthed 'Over there' and nodded to a door which was slightly ajar.

The door opened fully and I saw Cis standing with a face like thunder. Like me, she'd arrived earlier than planned and had observed my entire performance. Stunned, I just wished the ground would open and swallow me up. You see, Cis had a reputation as a real tough cookie and I thought to myself 'This is it, I'm for the chop even before we open.' Cis beckoned me over. As I stood in front of her, fearing the admonishment I was about to receive, she said, 'Hmm. I've got a great idea, why don't you do me in the show?'

'What do you mean, do YOU in the show?' I asked, quite puzzled.

'Well, do exactly what you just did. Didn't you see the reaction? It would be fantastic in the show!'

I felt as though I'd been spared from the guillotine. My blood circulated again and I resumed breathing. I was very slim at the time so Cis suggested I'd need to 'pad up a bit'; I was game for anything if it kept her sweet and me in the production. We used her original dress from the Novello show, to which I added a blonde wig and padding. I then performed the number again and she absolutely loved it. It went straight into our show, mercifully going down an absolute storm with audiences night after night.

As I mentioned, Cis had a reputation for being tough and a bit of a taskmaster but in all honesty she was absolutely delightful to me. I remember one day she asked, 'What are you doing for your birthday?' I wasn't sure how she even knew it *was* my birthday, but told her I'd made no plans as we'd just opened in the show. The next thing I know she'd booked a table at Quaglino's, my favourite restaurant, and threw an absolutely wonderful birthday dinner for me. She couldn't have been kinder, and even told me 'You're an absolute pleasure to work with, and there is hope for the theatre if other up-and-coming young actors have your attitude.'

With this ring

The weeks raced by and I have to say it was an absolutely joyous experience, perhaps made even more so by thoughts of my impending wedding day. Leigh had arranged for us to be married at Westminster Register Office and then to go on honeymoon straight afterwards to New York. However, the theatre management went back on their word and decided, because I was 'irreplaceable' in the show, that I shouldn't be allowed any time off after all.

Leigh was absolutely furious and told me to leave everything to him. He thought he'd play them at their own game and contacted

Love and Marriage

Sam Chase, his New York associate at *Billboard*, to see if he could come up with anything to give us some leverage. Sam said he had contacts at CBS and could wangle an appearance on a popular American TV show called *Bride and Groom*, where real-life couples got hitched live on television.

'But what use would that be to us in London?' Leigh asked.

'Look,' said Sam, 'forget getting married in London. Come over and get married in New York. I'll get you featured on the show afterwards, and you'll have more publicity than you'll know what to do with.'

It was a ratings-winning show, and though not screened in the UK it was beginning to makes waves – of disapproval – here, too. Consequently, it was making headlines. To my utter amazement, management said 'OK' to our week off. Since we'd received an 'official invitation' from CBS, they obviously thought they'd reap the benefits and could ride on the publicity when I returned.

Sam said we'd be featured as a newly married couple; we would fly to New York, get married at a place of our choice, have a nice break, then do the show and all the publicity, with *all* our expenses taken care of.

'Great,' I said, 'problem solved.' Or so I thought.

No sooner had we arrived at the hotel in New York than there was a knock at the door. 'Miss Gayson, we are here to measure you up for your wedding gown for the show,' the two dress designers exclaimed as they brushed past me into our room.

Confused, I asked Leigh to call Sam and see what the hell was going on. Sam admitted he hadn't quite told Leigh everything because if he had we might have refused to travel. He wouldn't say any more, other than 'All will be explained.'

The next thing we knew, the phone rang; it was the TV network. 'Well, of course you have to have a gown, you are getting married live on TV in a little chapel we've built inside the television studio.'

'What?!?'

I was furious!

Sam had sold us to the network as a 'famous London couple who wanted to marry live on air'. But what could we do? Return to London unmarried and risk the wrath of management? Marry in New York at a low-key ceremony of our own organisation and not get any publicity? No. Realising we were faced with a fait accompli there wasn't much we could do other than go along with it.

I did, however, ensure that it was going to be a legal marriage. I didn't want to go through all this and find out that the whole thing was a total sham just for the cameras. I insisted that we be married by an English chaplain; it was duly arranged for Claudius Kulow of the English Lutheran Church in St Albans to fly out and marry us – live on television. That was a first for the English church, and of course generated quite a few early headlines back home, much to the delight of the theatre management.

Sam called again, telling us not to worry about publicity as the programme was reaching at least three million people in the US and would certainly spill over onto UK screens too. 'Everything will be fine, enjoy your gifts.'

'Gifts?' I asked.

Sure enough, packages started to arrive: beautiful leather luggage with gold-plated handles, clothes, jewels, engagement rings and even furniture. Imagine trying to get that lot on a plane! As we had most of our own back in London we politely refused; our ingratitude didn't go down very well with the sponsors. Well, let me tell you, I was none too happy at the thought of these people trying to get in on my wedding!

I suppose the idea was that I'd wear their clothes and rings on air, and then lean back on the furniture posing for wedding photos, before jetting off on honeymoon with our luggage – and thus generating lots of lovely advertising for the sponsors.

Love and Marriage

We rehearsed for 45 minutes in the studio before the show went live on air. The first 15-minute segment of the programme featured Leigh and I being interviewed about our relationship before they cut to a commercial break; the scene then switched to a kitchen set where a cookery expert showed viewers how to make biscuits using Betty Crocker Pie Crust Mix (chief sponsor of the extravaganza). Meanwhile we were whisked to the chapel set for our English wedding ceremony. He said 'I do,' so did I, and we then returned to a living room set where we were showered with all the other wretched gifts we'd initially refused!

As we left the studios we were swamped by dozens of journalists and photographers, all clambering for our story. Little did we know that our 15 minutes of fame would cause an absolute stink at home in England. You see, commercial TV sponsorship deals were a hot topic and the British Parliament were debating the bill while being battered by anti-commercial opinions from the clergy and education sector, all citing that it was an example of 'bad taste' which might 'end the British way of life'. And our marriage was highlighted as a prime example.

Back at the hotel the phone never stopped ringing, with English journalists trying to get the scoop. It was beginning to get out of hand and Leigh, who hated not being in control, suggested we get back to England as soon as possible and face them on our own terms. We landed in London the next day and were greeted by what seemed like hundreds of journalists and photographers; it was an absolute bun fight and I wondered what on earth we'd walked into. The press wanted every single morsel of gossip and accused us of planning the whole thing to coincide with the parliamentary debate. What absolute rubbish!

So what started as a wheeze to get a week off, and generate a bit of publicity in return, turned out to be a weeks-on-end nightmare of hounding by the press. My new agent, Robin Fox at MCA, said, 'Look on the bright side, at least you're now a household name.'

I was quite well known before all of this but now I couldn't even leave our house in Green Street without being mobbed by photographers; it was horrid. The producers of *Over the Moon* didn't mind of course, as I was front page news and advance ticket sales went through the roof. Everyone wanted to come and see the 'publicity-crazed monster' who had caused a massive furore in Parliament.

I grew so weary of explaining what had happened, or rather trying to explain, that Leigh told me just to forget it. All that mattered was that we were finally married, so that was my answer to everything and everyone.

Making another impression

Back in *Over the Moon*, and looking for new characters to skit, Cis heard I did quite a good impersonation of Tallulah Bankhead. She asked me to show her and immediately put it in the revue. Bankhead, by the way, was an American actress renowned for her sexy deep voice and flamboyant personality, which I'd managed to get down to a tee. Jack Hulbert, the director, promised he'd have a song written but didn't feel there was any urgency and when I'd been told 'Not to worry' for the nth time I decided to take matters into my own hands. I found the perfect slinky dress and a composer friend wrote a song in Bankhead's style and we were all set to go with virtually no rehearsal time. I'd be opening live as Miss Bankhead that very evening.

Why am I telling you this? Well, slow dissolve to when *Over the Moon* finally finished its run. Leigh had planned a business trip to New York so I decided to tag along with him and make it the honeymoon we'd never had, plus it had the added advantage of getting us away from the UK media.

My agent, Robin at MCA, hooked me up with the New York office, where I was invited to a meeting. 'I understand you did an impersonation of Tallulah Bankhead which went down rather well, so I'd like to introduce you to a client of mine,' he said.

The door opened and in walked Miss Bankhead herself. I could feel my heart pounding out of my chest.

'Hello, I'm Tallulah Bankhead. I hear you mimicked me in your London revue?' she said in her deep voice.

'Well, I did my best, but you're a one-off,' I replied nervously, edging backwards.

'Yes, I am, aren't I?' She wasn't short of self-confidence!

Like Cis, her fiery reputation for not suffering fools was well known and I thought, 'This is it, she's going tear a strip off me.' But instead she said 'I'd like you to do it for me, now.'

Panic set in. I thought I was going to just die on the spot, with my heart pounding ever harder. 'What, here? Now?' I asked.

She nodded affirmatively, so I pulled myself together and thought if it worked for Cis it could work for Bankhead. I went ahead and did it. She paused for a second, then roared with laughter. 'Oh my God,' she said. 'Oh, that's great! You could have exaggerated a little more in places, but I'm glad you didn't actually.'

She hugged me and said, 'I hope we get to work together on something,' and with that left. I wonder if she'd have chased me out of town had she not approved? This business sure is a strange one.

Leigh and I meanwhile stayed in New York for a few days, where I was introduced to some producers and directors, before flying on to LA where Leigh was doing some writing for a production company; his career was now moving from journalism towards penning scripts. In fact, he later became a very successful writer (and producer) both in the UK and US on shows like *The Avengers*, *The Saint*, *Mission: Impossible*, *Fantasy Island* and *Hart to Hart*.

Dial 999

Back in London, formidable husband-and-wife team Sydney and Muriel Box were putting together a film called *Street Corner*. They were both previously involved with the running of Gainsborough Studios but after achieving huge success with *The Seventh Veil*, for which they won the Best Screenplay Oscar in 1947, they'd moved to Rank before becoming independents again. Though both still worked as writers, Sydney served primarily as a producer and Muriel as one of the only female directors in the business.

Muriel was always very keen to highlight women as the heroes of her films and with *Street Corner* she not only offered an alternative to the hugely popular *The Blue Lamp* but also emphasised the importance of women in the police force. Personally, I always thought it was a very bad title as it made us sound like hookers!

I played a policewoman called Janet. There was a good mix of old mates in there, including Michael Medwin and Dora Bryan, though alas it is not a particularly wonderful film, despite being shot in a semi-documentary style. The best thing to come out of it was that I made some lifelong friends in Barbara Murray and particularly Peggy Cummins.

Peggy has been so many things to me; friend, neighbour and co-star. At one point she lived next door to me in Mayfair. Back then she was married to Derek Dunnett, who was the son of the Carters' Seeds people. I remember one weekend, Peggy decided her father-in-law's grounds near London would be a great place to have a picnic followed by a firework display. It was where they grew all the rare plants for their seeds, in acres and acres of hothouses. As dusk fell, Derek produced a huge box and one by one we started letting off fireworks. They were all very colourful but when one went, with a life of its own, straight through the main hothouse roof, our first reaction was to run away like naughty children.

I stopped and asked Derek, 'What are you going to do?'

Realising the hugely damaging effect it would have on the business, he said 'My father will never forgive me for this.' He called the fire brigade anonymously and we sloped back to London, hoping they were able to limit the damage; however, the newspapers the next day reported that 'some idiots or children' had seriously damaged the Carters' Seeds main hothouse, plunging the company into difficulties. Poor Derek had to go to his father and confess everything. I don't think their relationship ever really recovered afterwards. Sadly, Derek is no longer with us, but I see Peggy every now and then and we reminisce ... about everything bar fireworks!

Though Leigh and I were on the whole very happy together, even as newlyweds some cracks in our relationship began to form. One of our biggest problems was the fact that we hardly ever saw each other. Leigh's work was taking him all over the world and my acting career was really blossoming, so finding time together was a rarity. My marriage was very important so I considered retirement, but Leigh would have none of it. He said my career was paramount to me, and going far too well to think about giving it all up.

But although he said one thing, he did another. You see, Leigh was a very jealous and *very* possessive man. When he was away I'd often have to attend premieres or make personal appearances. On one occasion I asked an actor friend of mine (a purely platonic friendship, I might add) if he'd join me as I hated turning up alone to these things. When Leigh found out he was absolutely furious and accused me of having an affair. I explained to him over and over that I couldn't bear to go alone and reassured him that the thought of cheating had never crossed my mind. But no matter how much I tried he wouldn't accept it, which understandably resulted in a lot of tension developing between us.

When my US agent secured the offer of a lucrative film contract in America, Leigh said he couldn't stand the idea of me being so far away for two or three years when his career in the UK was burgeoning. In particular, my getting attention from 'those

Hollywood types' was something he could not bear to think about. So I turned the contract down.

Fairbanks

Leigh was happy for me to have a career, but he wanted it to be one which fitted in with him, which was quite impossible. Then, in 1954, I thought all my prayers had been answered when Leigh landed the job of script editor on a TV series called *Douglas Fairbanks Jr Presents*, which would be filmed at Elstree Studios, north of London.

One particular story had a really meaty female role and Fairbanks asked Leigh if he knew anyone who could handle it. Of course he suggested me and, after showing Fairbanks some recent film footage, I was hired. Perfect, I thought – together at last.

Sadly, the reality was quite different. When I was filming all day at the studio, Leigh would be at home writing and editing the scripts. It was great for me on a professional level; the shows were American-financed and were broadcast in primetime slots in the States. As they seemed to like my work, I'd always be cast if a suitable part came up. So I guess it doesn't harm to have a script editor for a husband.

The shows were extremely popular, running from 1953 to 1957, and starred such household names as Christopher Lee, Honor Blackman and of course Douglas Fairbanks Jr himself, who appeared in 48 of the 117 episodes. It was a very happy time in my professional life, and though I didn't get to see Leigh at the studio that much, at least we were both in the same city and got to spend our evenings together.

The ball and chain

Many considered Leigh's attitude towards me sweet and touching. But he treated me like a delicate china doll, always calling me his 'baby', which I absolutely hated. I said, 'I'm your wife, not your baby.' He said it was just a term of endearment but the issues went much deeper and he started becoming totally over-protective in every aspect of my life. I was even forbidden to drive as he was terrified I'd end up in some fatal accident, so I had my own driver to take me down to the local shops.

He hated the idea that I might ever become self-sufficient and so made me feel totally insecure about trying to manage on my own. I wasn't allowed to answer the phone, open letters, pay bills, arrange repairs, or even organise nights out with friends without his say-so.

When I first met Leigh I was living with my mother, who took care of all the day-to-day admin duties like paying the electricity and gas bills. In fact, she was even my personal secretary at one point, organising just about everything in my life. So, naturally, when Leigh and I moved in together, I was quite happy that he and the housekeeper assumed that role. In hindsight I foolishly became totally dependent on them.

Though I was much more savvy later on in my career, my ever-increasing workload necessitated I recruit some help occasionally, so I asked my sister Patricia to become my personal secretary (the best secretary I could have asked for), while my mother handled my considerable fan mail. Otherwise, the lesson I learnt from being too dependent on Leigh was a well-heeded one and has stayed with me to this day.

By the way, Leigh was also a staunch vegetarian, and fully expected me to follow suit. I told him I didn't mind eating the odd veggie meal but converting completely was out of the question. So when he hired someone to prepare our meals, to save his 'baby' having to cook, and I discovered that she was a vegetarian chef – I really couldn't believe it.

Visiting friends for dinner was a painful experience as Leigh would announce, 'You do know we are vegetarians and cannot eat any meat or fish whatsoever.' It often became a real issue for our hosts as they would have to then prepare another dish, having previously thought I was a meat eater – which I was.

Then there was the subject of alcohol. I have never been a drinker except for the occasional glass of wine with dinner. Alcohol was an absolute no-no for Leigh; he was tee-total and would always preach, 'Wine is full of harmful ingredients and I am simply protecting you against yourself.' Friends would come over for dinner and question why I would be sipping orange juice instead of drinking the fine Chianti they were offered.

As time went on it became more and more of a problem. My doctor advised me that, as I was working at such a pace, I needed protein and therefore should eat more red meat. I told Leigh, thinking he would relent, but of course he knew best and dismissed the advice as poppycock. I was so furious with him one evening that I jumped in our Jaguar and drove out of town to a little restaurant I knew, and enjoyed a *huge* steak and half a bottle of Valpolicella. I knew I'd have to face the music when I returned home but I'd just about had enough!

When I got back to London, Leigh went absolutely ballistic, screaming, 'Where the hell have you been? I've been worried sick and was just about to call the police and report you missing.'

So much for married bliss!

Chapter Four

Joining the Ranks

In January 1953 I was offered a revue at the New Lindsey Theatre with Joan Sims, Ron Moody and Dilys Laye. *Intimacy at Eight* was so successful that the following year the producers said, 'We've put together another show and are thinking of calling it *More Intimacy at Eight*.' So I joined forces with Ron and Joan again. The producers then suggested we might come together for *Intimacy at Eight Thirty*. 'Where will all this intimacy end?' I wondered.

I next made a film called *Dance Little Lady* which was directed by Val Guest and shot out at Nettlefold Studios in Walton-on-Thames. The story was about a successful dancer's (Mai Zetterling) fight with her husband (Terence Morgan) for the attention of their daughter, as played by Mandy Miller, who had scored a tremendous success a couple of years earlier in a film called *Mandy*, which was about a disturbed little deaf girl. She was a very talented actress, but her father was concerned that she continued with her school studies and, though she appeared in several more films and TV shows, she 'retired' aged 18 to start a family life.

Dance Little Lady marked the first time, in my experience, that there had been a single seven-minute take in a British film. I know Hitchcock did it in America with *Rope*, but Val Guest wanted to experiment and asked me if I was up for it. I said, 'Yes, if we can rehearse it all thoroughly first.' We rehearsed all day and every mark had to be hit dead on; it was a very complicated scene, in and out of rooms and corridors, but Val was adamant there should be no cuts or close-ups, just one mid-angled take. The camera operator and our lighting cameraman, Wilkie Cooper, both said it couldn't be done and were concerned about the lights as well as the sound, but Val brought in the art director, Fred Pusey, and explained how he wanted the set to open up and where the camera tracks were to be laid.

At the end of the day's rehearsal we were absolutely exhausted, but we shot the scene in one take!

I played a ballerina, Adele. Though I had done some dancing the only point work I'd ever done was in panto in the mid-1940s, so they brought in Nadia Nerina, who was the prima ballerina at Sadler's Wells. She danced for some of my scenes and I had to just come in on point in close-up, but boy did my toes and feet hurt; in fact, they drew blood at one point. It just shows what real ballerinas have to go through.

Guess who?

Next I appeared in the BBC drama *Men of Mystery* before opening a new series called *Guess My Story*, which aired on the BBC every Sunday evening; this was my first of many appearances. It was similar in format to *What's My Line?* but this time a panel of celebrities, including Elizabeth Allan, Rikki Fulton, Peter Jones and myself, interrogated a member of the public who had recently featured in the news for one reason or another. I hit the jackpot on my first ever guess after noticing the contestant had rather dirty fingernails; imagine my surprise when he confirmed my suspicions that he was actually a dustman! I went on to another three successful guesses out of a possible eight. How about that?

One of the most memorable episodes featured The Crazy Gang as celebrity guests and, boy, did they live up to their name. No matter what question I asked, those scoundrels did their very best to wind me up. I'd get Bud Flanagan and Jimmy

Joining the Ranks

Nervo answering yes and no simultaneously for example, and their constant silliness resulted in me getting, visibly, quite annoyed. I feigned my best showbiz smile but yearned for the end of transmission and the safety of my dressing room. We were, by the way, supposed to be guessing The Crazy Gang's secret dream, but the whole thing had been a set-up right from the start. No matter what, we were destined to fail in our attempts to solicit answers.

The host, Peter West, declared, 'All prices must come down with a bang!' On the word 'bang', The Crazy Gang pulled a rope and the whole panel was showered with flour and God knows what else. Elizabeth Allan was so furious that she threw a glass of water at Peter West. I, meanwhile, was wearing a beautiful diamond tiara which ended up askew and covered in gunk, while Peter Jones and Rikki Fulton's beautifully cut suits were totally ruined. Eventually our anger turned to smiles as we joined in with the tomfoolery, throwing handfuls of flour at our rather mischievous guests. Talk about an act bringing the roof down.

At the time the press made a huge issue of my apparent rivalry with Elizabeth Allan on the programme, suggesting we would try and outdo each other with our jewellery each episode; one headline read 'The struggle for sparkle'. Honestly, how ridiculous. Mind you, it's no less trivial than some of the news stories that are in the papers these days. It just shows that, where the press are concerned, nothing really changes.

Meanwhile, in April 1954 the BBC launched Britain's first ever soap opera, *The Grove Family*, so named after its Lime Grove Studios, and in July I was invited to guest in one of the episodes. I can't recall my character, but I do remember the lovely cast, including Christopher Beeny, Edward Evans and Margaret Downs. Within a year they were commanding audiences of nine million, all tuning in to see the trials and tribulations of this middle-class family. Even the Queen Mother was a big fan.

Danzigers

For their early B-movies and TV series the Danziger brothers, Edward and Harry, leased space from various studios before deciding to build their own base in Elstree in 1955 – New Elstree Studios. There they gave breaks to actors such as Gordon Jackson, Laurence Payne, Francis Matthews, Anton Rodgers, Nyree Dawn Porter, Jill Ireland and Peter Butterworth.

To be honest, most of their output was fairly cheap, often made on a shoestring budget and ridiculously short shooting schedules. I remember we had two and a half days for one TV show I made there, and I was told by colleagues that they'd maybe have a couple of weeks for a feature film, but that was luxury. If they ever fell behind schedule, the director was told to literally rip out a page or two from the script. Other stories circulated that US networks would never buy anything that looked arty, and so photography had to be good and well lit; bugger the scripts, as long as they looked OK! Oh, and male actors were never to wear bow ties on screen, as US audiences would assume the characters were 'goddam faggots', the brothers said.

A lot of actors looked down their noses at the Danzigers. Some only took roles because their dressing rooms had telephones, enabling them to call round about other jobs, but others were simply pleased to accept work with up-and-coming directors. If a job was offered, I never turned it away without good reason. *The Vise*, hosted by Australian actor Ron Randell, was a crime and mystery series with a twist at the end similar to *Douglas Fairbanks Presents*. They made two episodes a week, then, at the end of 1955, it switched format and became a mystery series featuring the private investigations of former Scotland Yard Inspector Mark Saber, played by Donald Gray.

Although I don't recall anything too exciting I appeared in three episodes, two of which were directed by David MacDonald, and I remember Bryan Forbes co-starred in one of them.

Joining the Ranks

What with *The Vise, Douglas Fairbanks Presents, The Grove Family* and *Men of Mystery* I found myself on television quite a lot that year. Unfortunately it didn't pay a fortune, but the notoriety it brought was huge. So much so I received an offer from the Rank Organisation.

Signing with Rank

Rank was by far the biggest player in the British film industry, with its studios and production unit out at Pinewood, its distribution business, its ownership of Odeon cinemas and of course its famous 'Company of Youth' or (as we all knew it) The Rank Charm School, from which the likes of Joan Collins, Christopher Lee and Anthony Steel graduated. Rank had a number of stars under contract, including Diana Dors, Kenneth More, Dirk Bogarde, Donald Sinden and Norman Wisdom, along with a great many top film-makers such as Roy Ward Baker, Ken Annakin, Ralph Thomas, Betty Box and Lewis Gilbert.

Anyhow, in 1955 Rank contacted my agent, Robin Fox at MCA, and said they had some scripts that they would be very interested in talking to me about. Robin explained they were offering me the chance of a very big contract and leading roles. I naturally spoke with Leigh, who wisely said 'Let's see the scripts first.' They sent a few, and I thought all of them were very good with nice parts. In those days roles for women were usually terrible; they were either housewife or landlady character parts, or frightfully posh with the little chastity rose between the bosoms, and if you didn't fit into either of those categories you didn't get cast.

Leigh and Robin both thought the deal was a good one, and would make me the highest paid actress on Rank's books. I signed a seven-year contract.

'You'll be starring in your own films now,' Robin said confidently.

Rank made one stipulation: I wasn't allowed to do any television. But I didn't mind, as obviously I was now earning a regular salary, regardless of whether I was working or not, and so I wouldn't need to take on any other jobs. TV was actually considered a huge threat to cinema with its growing popularity, and relative affordability, effectively stopping people going to the cinema for their news and entertainment fix. This understandably worried the Rank Organisation greatly; so much so, they set about 'removing' the most popular dramatic actors and actresses from television by offering them film contracts. Their plan was to 'eliminate the competition'.

After six months I hadn't made a single film with Rank, though I did just about everything else, from having scores of publicity stills taken with Cornel Lucas, reading script after script they sent me, and being rented out to advertising companies endorsing everything from hairgrips to car seat covers, Ronson lighters, ironing boards, coffee, furniture ranges and even toothbrushes! Then there were the public appearances – judging beauty contests, dog shows, opening fêtes and attending film festivals.

Where's Ava?

That reminds me, in August 1955 I was dispatched to the Venice Film Festival along with most of the British stalwarts of the Rank stable, including Belinda Lee, Diana Dors, Claire Bloom, Jack Hawkins, John Gregson, Donald Sinden, James Robertson Justice, director Ralph Thomas, studio head John Davis and his wife Dinah Sheridan. Rank really were flying the flag and pushing the boat out; rather aptly, too, as their big film screening was *Doctor At Sea*.

Soon after our arrival, Theo Cowan, who was the head of publicity for Rank at that time, said, 'There's a big party of foreign press at the airport today; a lot of the American stars are arriving. I've fixed up for you, Diana Dors and Claire Bloom to get over there earlier because we want a story to push the American stars off the front pages.'

Joining the Ranks

So we all arrived at the airport, dressed up to the nines naturally, and were paraded as the top British stars. Thankfully the American plane was coming in late, so we did our photo shoot without interruption or distraction. Now, Ava Gardner was due on the American plane. However, she'd meanwhile had a bust up with Frank Sinatra (their rows were apparently legendary) and he'd said, 'You're not getting on that plane.' No one Stateside had bothered to tell the people in Venice that Ava wasn't coming. Consequently, a huge bank of new photographers had now surged into the airport to photograph Ava arriving. Being curious, we went to see what was happening and the next thing I knew somebody thrust a microphone in my face and said in a very heavy Italian accent, 'Welcome to Venice, Miss Gardner.' I looked nothing like Ava Gardner apart from being dark and slender.

I don't know what made me do it but I put on my best American accent and said, 'Oh, it's just lovely to be here in Venice and, oh, the weather's as beautiful as in LA.'

I didn't care what rubbish I came out with, thinking it all a giggle, but my little joke got out of hand, as all the journalists started questioning me about the state of my marriage to Sinatra.

'Oh well, you know this kinda thing happens,' I said. 'You don't want to believe everything you read in the press and excuse me for saying so but you can be very naughty.' I thought, 'I'm getting deeper and deeper here', and heard Theo saying 'For God's sake get her off.'

A journalist said, 'Apparently Sinatra has said you're through. What's your comment on this, Miss Gardner?' 'I do hope not, nobody wants a failed marriage and nobody likes to fail, do they?' What the hell was I saying? I thought, 'Ava's going to kill me when she hears this.'

I just carried on with this inane chatter! Then I said, 'Oh, I'm so sorry, but as you know the flight was delayed and I'm a bit late and the car's waiting. Thank you so much for being patient for so long and I hope I get to you see you again during the festival.'

Theo grabbed me. 'I nearly had a heart attack. What the hell are you doing to me, Eunice?'

'Well, they were convinced I was Ava. What could I do?'

Fortunately my suitably vague comments didn't really interest the press, and so Diana Dors and I got all the publicity for Rank after all!

Pulling Rank

Back home, I told Leigh that I was getting worried about the Rank deal and getting fed up with doing everything but acting, so we called a meeting with the Rank management and asked when the films they promised would be starting. They gave all sorts of excuses about scripts needing changes, and not to worry as there were a lot of new stories and projects in the pipeline for me. Reassured, I continued opening fêtes and turning up to functions where I was always described, for the news cameras, as 'Rank contract star Eunice Gayson'.

By about the tenth month there still wasn't a film in sight and I'd really had enough. Prior to signing with Rank, I was sometimes asked to make public appearances and on one occasion was paid £1000. I then totted up all the gigs I'd done for Rank, and worked out that my salary from them equated to a fraction of the potential single appearance fees. I wouldn't have minded if I'd been making films and furthering my career, but I wasn't. Adding insult to injury, my agent had turned away several good TV series and a lucrative cabaret stint in Las Vegas, all because of this blessed contract.

I called a crisis meeting with MCA. They said the only thing to do was threaten to pull the plug. Robin Fox told me that he thought I'd been set up; it happened to another actor he represented who had done very well on television. They'd sent me scripts knowing full well they would never be made. Rank's reaction was to tell me they were readying a film called *House of Secrets* in which I was to play second female lead behind Julia Arnall.

Now I'm not immodest, but Julia Arnall was a model and recent Charm School graduate with about four bit-part credits to her name before making her acting debut proper in *Lost* the year before. They were expecting me to take billing below her, and to play a tiny supporting role. Where were the leading parts I'd been promised?

I said, 'I'm leaving.'

'We'll sue you,' they responded.

'And I'll sue you, as I now realise this was a scam. You had no intention of using me in films but just wanted to keep me off TV.'

One year on from signing, I tore up the contract. Rank didn't sue me, but they did issue a press statement.

'Miss Eunice Gayson, the film actress, has been released from her contract with the Rank Organisation,' it said. 'The decision was taken although important parts had been earmarked for her this year. We are now choosing another actress for the role she was to have had in *House of Secrets*, work on which is to begin in a few weeks.'

Ealing

With Rank firmly behind me, I was next offered a job at Ealing Studios, which was of course synonymous with the famous comedies of the 1940s and '50s such as *Kind Hearts And Coronets* and *The Ladykillers*. Michael Balcon, who ran the company, also produced a great number of what I call flag-waving films; he was a huge patriot and during the war made many important morale-boosting movies such as *Went The Day Well?* His patriotism continued in the post-war years and extended to the air travel industry.

I'd met Balcon a few years before. I think it might have been at an audition. Anyhow, my abiding memory of him was of him saying, very matter of factly: 'I would love to use you but would you please do something about your right eyebrow? Surely you must have heard other people saying that to you? It's so suggestive. You can say hello to somebody but the eyebrow says something else!'

Talk about giving me a complex! I remember thinking I'd never work for Michael Balcon, but I was offered the part of Penny Henson in *Out of the Clouds*, a semi-documentary style movie to be produced by Balcon and directed by Basil Dearden. The Ministry of Transport and Civil Aviation offered huge support (in fact it was one big advertisement for them) and set up production offices for us at London Airport, now known as Heathrow. However, the huge interior of the terminal building was recreated at Ealing Studios, becoming one of the largest sets ever constructed there.

The film was quite episodic, with a number of small stories featuring various characters all coming together as a whole. I shared most of my scenes with Anthony Steel. The most noteworthy thing to report about the whole experience was that I was responsible for introducing Tony to Anita Ekberg. Anita was in London receiving huge press coverage; everybody was talking about this beautiful girl. Tony said, 'I hear you're going to make a film called *Zarak* with her. I want to meet her.'

I said, 'Look, I know what you're like – you love them and leave them.'

'Yes, but I have a feeling about this girl. I *really* want to meet her.'

I introduced them at the Dorchester bar and I've never seen such electricity between two people. She turned to me and asked excitedly, 'What have you done?'

Tony said, 'My God, I was right.'

Anita was a very interesting lady – very fulsome, very buxom and very gorgeous in a Swedish way which Tony liked. She'd been out in Hollywood, and under contract to Howard Hughes' RKO

Pictures. In fact, she said Hughes was fixated and wanted to marry her, but when the contract led nowhere she left. It's a pity I didn't listen to her stories about Hughes a little more closely, as you'll find out in the next chapter.

Tony and Anita fell madly in love with each other and, sure enough, they were married soon after. But of course they later realised that, when the initial wild amore calmed, things weren't all rosy in the garden. What's more they blamed me for introducing them!

Anita went back to live in Rome and had a good career for a time, and lots of boyfriends too, I believe. Tony followed her, which did his career no good whatsoever, and they divorced after just three years of marriage. He then made some European B-movies and was often referred to as Mr Ekberg, later punctuating the odd TV role with otherwise forgettable films – some being soft porn. He disappeared off the radar totally in the 1980s, but a decade or so later a Sunday newspaper ran a story about Tony and how he was living in a council flat in West London, penniless and a total recluse. Fortunately, his old agent read the piece and contacted the paper to say he was holding residual cheques for Tony and asked if they'd put him in touch.

With a little money behind him, and a little help, Tony then moved into the actors' retirement home and even did the odd TV show again. He died in 2001.

Back to *Out of the Clouds*. It was lovely to be working again with James Robertson Justice, who was an absolute pussycat, he really was. He always played the tumultuous character and his career became dependent on this to a huge extent, but he couldn't have been more different in private.

Sadly, the reverse was true of our director Basil Dearden, who was, as far as I was concerned, quite a horrible man. I'd never worked for him before but had been impressed by his earlier credits, including a Will Hay film. But one morning I heard this muttering going on in the dressing room next to mine and as it grew in intensity I distinctly heard the voice say, 'What makes you think you're an actor? Oh, you've been told it, have you? Well, I'm a director and I don't see any sign of it and I wonder why the hell I cast you in the first place.'

I looked round the door and saw Dearden sitting in front of the mirror. I thought, 'If he's rehearsing that, I'd better look on the call sheet to see what he was shooting.' Along with my scenes, there were some with Bernard Lee, who was one of one Britain's most experienced character actors.

I asked Bernie if he'd had any trouble with Basil and he said he found him 'weird and hard to reach out to'. I told him what I'd heard and warned Bernie he could be in the firing line. Surprise, surprise: Dearden came on set, called Bernie to one side and gave him the previously rehearsed 'What makes you think you're an actor?' tirade.

Bernie lost his temper and walked off the set. Michael Balcon ordered him back, but Bernie said, 'Would you like to tell the director that personal remarks are not necessary? I've been in this business most of my life and I've never been spoken to like that before.' Balcon had words, and we continued in what was a really frosty atmosphere, causing me to certainly raise my eyebrow at times!

As for this being a potential return to the screen after Rank... Well, I'm afraid Dearden's wife, Melissa Stribling, was in the film and most of his attention was focused on making her look good, over and above the rest of the cast. Consequently, it doesn't rate as one of my favourite films I'm afraid.

The road to Morocco

Pillage, plunder and passion! Or so proclaimed the poster for the feature film *Zarak*, which was loosely based on the 1949 book *The*

Left: My beautiful mother, Mary Elizabeth Sargaison, who earned the nickname 'Billie the Peach'.

Above: Brother Kenneth dotes over his twin sisters, after initially being horrified we weren't baby boys!

Below: Although twins, I was always taller and bigger than Pat.

Right and below: Now a teenager, here I am with Mother and Pat – on holiday and at home.

Opposite top: One of my first TV appearances was in *The Teenage Show* for the BBC, transmitted live from Alexandra Palace in 1948.

Opposite below left: When I signed a contract with Rank, I did everything but make movies – advertising hairgrips being one of my many endorsements!

Opposite below right: Taking a break at the Venice Film Festival, but the photographers were never far away.

Newey's
Blend Rite
BRITISH REGD. TRADE MARK
HAIR GRIPS

EUNICE GAYSON

THEY BLEND WITH YOUR HAIR
BRITISH PATENT No 425446

Supplied in

BLACK

BROWN

BLONDE

or GREY

MADE IN ENGLAND BY NEWEY BROS. LTD.

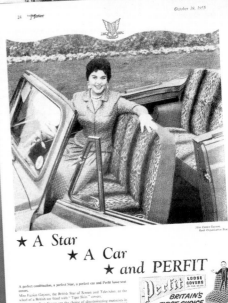

Opposite top: Cardew 'The Cad' Robinson in revue with me at The New Lindsey Theatre in 1951.

Opposite below left: *Dance Little Lady* was the first of a few happy collaborations with director Val Guest.

Opposite below right: Yet another Rank endorsement. Move over hair grips, hello car seat covers!

Left: After tearing up my Rank contract, I moved to Ealing Studios and made *Out of the Clouds* with Anthony Steel.

Below: Front page news!

Opposite: On location in Morocco for *Zarak*.

Inset top: My co-star in *Zarak*, the lovely Michael Wilding.

Inset middle: With Tom Conway in *The Last Man To Hang?*

Inset bottom: Drowning for real, in *Carry On Admiral*.

This page: *The Revenge of Frankenstein* was anything but horrific with the wonderful Peter Cushing and Richard Wordsworth (above), and Michael Gwynn (right).

PALACE THEATRE
SHAFTESBURY AVENUE · W.1   GERRARD 6834
Licensed by the Lord Chamberlain to and under the management of Emile Littler

THE
SOUND
OF
MUSIC

PROGRAMME—ONE SHILLING

"NO WAY TO STOP IT"   ELSA, THE CAPTAIN
                               AND MAX

Above: With Charles Chaplin Jr, my co-star in *Oh Men! Oh Women!*

Right: The Palace Theatre and *The Sound of Music* were the most wonderful six years of my life!

Joining the Ranks

Story of Zarak Khan by A J Bevan, set in the Northwest Frontier and Afghanistan. It was produced by Irving Allen and Albert R Broccoli's Warwick Film Productions.

Though one critic dismissed the film as 'a minor piece of escapism', I actually think this 99-minute adventure was rather good, and if nothing else it boasted a great cast and a surprising amount of emerging film talent. Ted Moore handled the Technicolor and CinemaScope photography superbly, later performing similar marvels on the early James Bond films. Art director John Box and costume designer Phyllis Dalton went on to win Oscars for their later work on *Doctor Zhivago*, while Richard Maibaum, who adapted the novel, went on to write scripts for *Dr No*, *From Russia With Love* and *Goldfinger*, among others. The director Terence Young and producer Albert R Broccoli would, of course, be instrumental in bringing the Bond movies to the big screen.

Major Michael Ingram was played by Michael Wilding and his co-stars included Victor Mature, Anita Ekberg and Patrick McGoohan. McGoohan played Moor Larkin, an adjutant to Wilding's character, who had a great love for billiards as well as offering sensible, albeit ignored, advice. His performance created a considerable stir in the popular British cinema magazine *Picturegoer*, where Margaret Hinxman – the doyenne of film critics – named McGoohan her 'Talent Spot'. She told her readers that this new face would be 'really something, given a half-decent part.' Though she completely slated the film itself, describing it as 'absurd'!

The film generated publicity in other quarters too when its poster was criticised by the House of Lords for 'bordering on the obscene' and was banned from being used as advertising in UK cinemas.

But I digress. I was cast as Cathy Ingram, the wife of Michael Wilding's character, and I greatly looked forward to the exciting location shoot out in North Africa – a far cry from the draughty sound stages back in England, and from the mundane work Rank had engaged me in.

My marriage to Leigh was in real trouble at this point and verging on collapse. I hoped our professional separation for a few weeks and the distance between us might help. But, typically not wanting to let his 'little baby' out of his sight, Leigh insisted he came to London Airport to see me off to Morocco. A loving gesture? Well yes, you'd think so, but as we were saying our goodbyes Leigh walked over to Victor Mature.

'Mr Mature, I'm entrusting this lady to your care,' he said. 'Just make sure everyone treats her with dignity. Any problems, here's my number.'

Now, the way Leigh said it was really more in the manner of 'This is my lady and I don't want to hear of anyone making a move on her.' I cringed. Mature, who you must remember was a huge star then and one with a bit of a reputation for the ladies, looked rather put out and asked me 'Who the hell is this guy?'

'He is my husband,' I replied sheepishly.

Mature paused for a moment, cracked a smile and said, 'Oh, how sweet. He cares so much for you.'

I breathed a sigh of relief and waved Leigh goodbye. I was so glad to get on that plane and away from the constant feeling of being smothered. I realised we couldn't go on, but really didn't know how to end it. At least I now had time to think.

Just as we were boarding, word came through that my costumes hadn't arrived from Berman's. A quick enquiry by phone and the response was that they thought 'Miss Gayson's costumes would not be needed just yet.' Not needed! Not needed? We were boarding the plane! They were beautiful Edwardian-style clothes and not ones you could readily pick up just anywhere. However, we were assured that they'd be ready the very next day.

Terence, ever the practical director, suggested I should stay back, because if I travelled and the clothes didn't follow the next day there would be no way of getting costumes in time. We had a better chance of finding replacements in London, which I'd need to be fitted for, so it was decided I'd stay behind and travel the next day, with my wardrobe.

Leigh was meanwhile overjoyed that he had his baby with him for an extra night. My expression must have said it all.

At the crack of dawn, the costumes arrived, thankfully, and I received the call to head to the airport again. There was no need for Leigh to warn off any co-stars this time. However, on the plane I was seated next to an extremely handsome man and I remember asking him, 'Are you an actor? If not you certainly should be.' Imagine Leigh overhearing that?

He was indeed an actor, named Macdonald Carey, and was flying to Morocco to star in a film called *Odongo* – also for Warwick Films. As we were just about to take off, he grabbed my hand forcefully. I said, 'Hang on, we might become friends but it doesn't extend to that.'

He sat rigidly in his seat and as I looked at him I could see he was absolutely terrified, in fact so terrified his nails dug into my hand and drew blood. He later apologised and said he was so pleased to be sitting next to someone who understood his fear of flying.

Take 1

On my first day of shooting I arrived on set in one of the beautiful (but delayed) costumes, and was welcomed by all the cast including Anita Ekberg, who came over and said, 'Oh darling, your clothes are magnificent and you look fabulous in them. It's just a shame they don't fit so well.'

'Fit so well?' I gasped.

I couldn't believe it; my clothes were an absolutely perfect fit. Talk about her getting off on the wrong foot on day one. I suspected she was going to be trouble!

Victor Mature on the other hand was terrific; he was a real gentleman and, as would please Leigh, was very protective, though not so much as to smother me. If someone said something curtly, or tried to upstage me, he kept his eye firmly on them and let his displeasure be known. When he finished filming each day he disappeared, not to be seen until make-up the next morning, and always looking as fresh as a daisy. Being a good girl I was tucked up in bed early ready for the next day as our calls were usually before 6.00 am.

I asked Victor what his secret was for looking so great at such an ungodly hour. 'I enjoy life, it's simple,' he replied.

No one really knew where he went but rumours were rife that he visited the Kasbah to partake of whatever delights were on offer! I'd often pull his leg and tell him that I'd ended up in some unsavoury situation the night before and that he wasn't there to protect me and of course I'd have to tell Leigh, but he would just laugh and change the subject.

Victor's method of acting was rather bizarre. Most actors learn their lines, then discuss them with the director – not Victor! He'd sit for hours reading his script, muttering, 'That's a five' or 'Oh, that's definitely an 18,' which was really puzzling. I asked Terence Young if he knew what was going on. 'It's the way he acts, he allocates a number to a particular line, the number relates to a certain look or attitude and he builds the scene around it,' he replied. It was a sort of acting by numbers technique.

That was all well and good, but Victor often couldn't remember what number he'd allocated to a particular line, so idiot boards were placed around the set to remind him. It was a bit off-putting for us actors; we'd be trying to make eye contact with him and he'd be glancing over our shoulders working out how he should deliver his next line.

Terence convinced me to go with it, and when we ran the rushes I thought, 'My God he was right.' You were entranced by Victor's performance and he blew everyone else away. From that day on, whenever I saw a Victor Mature film I couldn't help saying 'That's a 13' or 'That's definitely an eight.'

Of course, Victor started in the business as a stunt man. However, throughout this production he refused to do a single stunt, nor would he get on a horse unless there was a team of stunt men on hand to 'control the beast' – not that it *was* a beast! He told me this was because, many years earlier, on a previous movie he was thrown into a sheer drop by a horse and broke virtually every bone in his body, and was in hospital for months, costing him not only huge medical bills, but also future employment. So, understandably, I wasn't surprised by his stance.

But imagine our amazement when, on the last day, he dismissed the stunt man and said 'I'll handle this one.' Smiling wryly at Terence, he proceeded to pick up a heavy sideboard!

In the Kasbah

Before even a foot of film had been shot, one of our local production chaps gave us girls a pep talk about how to behave when visiting the Kasbah. 'You must *always* cover your face, *always* wear appropriate clothing and *never* go in alone, as if you do, the locals will think you are a whore and things could get very dangerous,' he said.

Of course, we all stuck by these simple rules... apart from one person. Yes, you guessed it, Anita Ekberg. She'd decided to not only visit the Kasbah alone but to wear the skimpiest of shorts and tightest of tops. The next thing we knew, our production chappie was rushing on set screaming, 'Come quick, come quick, Miss Ekberg is in *big* trouble.'

We all downed tools and followed him to the Kasbah, where we saw Ekberg fleeing for her life and screaming the place down, with several Arabs brandishing sticks and stones on her tail. They cornered her and began shouting 'whore, whore' as they crept in closer and closer. Ekberg looked terrified. Then Terence, who had a very commanding voice, pushed in and shouted 'Stop,' and to give him credit managed to calm the situation down by offering them money and promising that it would never happen again.

Ekberg was severely reprimanded and, despite being just a few weeks into the shoot, she was told she'd have to pack her bags and leave. You see, Cubby and Irving were informed by the local crew that her behaviour was 'totally unacceptable' and, if she didn't leave, they feared it might be difficult for the film to continue.

Terence said any scenes requiring her presence could be shot as inserts at the studio, and with that she was taken to the airport.

Fit for a Sultan

Almost every evening when I returned to the hotel, there would be a message saying that Leigh had called. It was nice to hear from him, but when he started expecting me to call him back every day... well, it became impossible as I'd have had to book a line hours in advance and even then I couldn't be sure of getting connected. I asked the concierge to tell him, when he called again, that we were filming and working very hard and that I sent all my love and would see him soon. But he still called and still left messages daily, hoping I'd call back as he 'missed hearing his baby's voice.' Argh!

I wasn't alone in my marital stress. Michael Wilding had brought his then wife, Elizabeth Taylor, along for the ride – not that you really knew it as she was always hidden away in the house they were renting while most of us cast and crew were staying at La Mamounia in Marrakesh. We'd heard that journalists from one of the Hollywood gossip magazines had been seen lurking around the set, trying to get any dirt they could on their relationship, which was rumoured to be on the rocks. What they didn't find they usually made up; it was even suggested that Taylor was having an affair with Victor Mature while Wilding was having an affair with Anita Ekberg. What rubbish!

Michael was often reprimanded for arriving late on set, but told us it was because Liz wouldn't allow him out of the house until she was fully made up, eyelashes, nails, hair... the lot.

'If she never leaves the house why does she feel the need to wear make-up and have her hair done?' I asked.

Although Liz modestly didn't consider herself one of the most beautiful women in the world, everyone else did, he explained. This way she would never be caught off guard without make-up, and so live up to the legend. One day, word came through that the local Sultan had invited us, and Liz, to his palace for supper. Such an invitation was considered a huge privilege and you could feel the excitement brewing as the day's filming came to an end. We were warned not to refuse any of the delicacies offered, as it would offend our host, and even though the food would be rather unconventional by Western standards it would, we were assured, be absolutely delicious.

We duly arrived at the magnificent palace and were ushered into a huge and lavish dining room, where giggling harem girls hid behind screens. The walls were adorned with the most beautiful fabrics imaginable, all finished with gold leaf; it was incredible – just like a film set. The Sultan, who sat at the end of an enormous dining table, welcomed us and introduced us to all the local dignitaries before instructing us to sit down and enjoy the food.

Glancing over the table in the hope of finding something familiar, I noticed a platter piled high with what looked like eyes. One of the dignitaries said, 'Sheep's eyes, delicious, delicious,' and signalled me to try.

Smiling nervously I popped one in my mouth, and was pleasantly surprised how nice they actually were, with a taste and texture very similar to mushrooms. The rest of the cast and crew, all initially hesitant, followed my lead and tucked in. That is to say all apart from Liz Taylor.

'If you think I'm eating sheep's eyeballs you can forget it,' she mouthed to Michael Wilding.

'Oh Liz, try them, they taste just like mushrooms,' I said, trying to encourage her not to offend our host. 'I hate mushrooms' was her curt reply.

Terence suggested she put the eye in her mouth then slip it into a napkin when the Sultan wasn't looking, and then pretend to chew. Realising we were all determined not to offend our host, this she did, but she couldn't resist going one better and proclaiming it the most delicious thing she had ever tasted which pleased the Sultan beyond measure. In fact, he called for more to be brought to our table!

Another local delicacy were fried ants; they were all dead but some of them honestly looked as though they were moving. Liz was feeling queasy enough as it was, but I quietly suggested she give them a try as they had a rather nice crunchy consistency. Of course she kicked up a huge fuss and refused to eat them, that is until she saw Terence's angry face staring back at her. He gestured at her napkin; she again pretended to eat them, but in fact hid them as before, while booming out, 'Oh my word, these are absolutely delicious.'

The Sultan smiled and clapped his hands. The ants were removed and, thinking they were the final course, Liz breathed a huge sigh of relief. Imagine her horror as another platter arrived containing sheep livers 'with a light sauce to help them slip down.'

By the end of the meal her napkin was positively bulging with food and she obviously needed to get rid of it all. Terence stood up, stretched his arms, and suggested Liz take some air with him. Pretending to admire the view, Liz flung the food into the courtyard below and returned to her seat, again proclaiming it was the most delicious meal she'd ever had. Talk about an Oscar-winning performance!

Out on location

By this time, Liz was getting bored to tears, as Michael was filming all day and she was hidden away from prying eyes back at the house, so not surprisingly word came through that she would be joining us for a location shoot up in the mountains. She felt it was isolated enough, away from the circling journalists. But Terence wasn't too happy to be honest, as the journey to the location was quite perilous; we had to walk, helping to carry equipment, most of the way. The last thing he wanted was a spectator and a potential insurance claim if anything happened.

We literally had to cross part of the Atlas mountains, and it was done with the aid of a Bailey bridge. The high winds made it sway, and despite our guides insisting it would be totally safe we were all rather trepidatious. As we were about half way across I heard a loud snapping noise; with a terrified look on his face our guide screamed, 'RUN, RUN!!!'

We all tore across to the other side and within a few seconds the bridge was left hanging in tatters, along with our nerves. Thankfully everyone was present and correct so we continued up the mountain. Well, we couldn't go back, could we?

We hadn't walked very far when a huge clap of thunder stopped us in our tracks, followed by the most torrential downpour of rain I've ever seen in my life. We were in the middle of nowhere and everyone was soaked to the skin.

Terence asked the guide if he had any ideas where we could shelter and keep the expensive equipment dry. He replied that there was a house quite close by which we could maybe use. By this time none of us actually cared, especially Liz Taylor, who wished she'd stayed back in the warmth and comfort of the house.

We walked along a narrow muddy path, looking like drowned rats, and sure enough came across a tiny, almost ramshackle hut, with white smoke billowing from its chimney. Terence banged on the door but there was no response. The pouring rain was so loud by now that I dare say anyone would have struggled to hear a knock on the door. He banged again and a voice from inside shouted, 'Go away and leave me alone.'

'We need your help,' Terence shouted back. 'We're a film crew and we are very wet and the ladies are very frightened; we just need somewhere to shelter and dry off.'

'Go away, you have no business here,' came the reply.

'I'll make it worth your while,' Terence called back.

The bolts on the door slid back and the door creaked open, revealing a rather dishevelled man. 'How?' he asked.

Terence offered him some dirham but he gestured for more, so Terence kept feeding him money until he finally invited us in. There was little in the way of comfort, with only two wooden benches to sit on, though we weren't complaining, just thankful to be out of the monsoon.

It was rather surreal that this old chap had some of the world's biggest film stars all huddled together in his bijou mountaintop house, jostling for a position near the fire, yet not knowing any of them. I remember thinking that it was lucky Anita Ekberg had been sent home – she was a rather buxom lady and would have taken up quite a lot of room around the fireplace!

The downpour continued for what seemed an eternity and our host was actually quite friendly, but maybe that was because he was expecting to relieve Terence of more money. I kept looking at him, thinking there was something very familiar about this guy but I couldn't quite put my finger on it. Then it clicked.

Slow dissolve...

When I was much younger, I was very close to my Uncle Harry (married to my mother's sister), who was a very tall chap with a deep resounding voice. I always remember thinking the voice suited him, as he was a barrister.

Harry had a twin brother called Willy who was never spoken of. I'm not sure I ever met him to be honest, but I do vaguely recall my mother telling me once, when I questioned his existence, that my Uncle Willy had 'gone away'.

'To prison?' I asked. 'A scandal in the family, how exciting,' I thought.

'No, not prison, he's just gone away,' she said, 'and we won't be talking about him again.'

Our mountain-top host reminded me greatly of Uncle Harry – he too was tall and had a deep voice. I don't quite know why, but I got it into my mind that he could be my long lost Uncle Willy. With my curiosity roused, I took him to one side.

'Excuse me, I think I know you,' I said.

He looked back at me very churlishly. 'I don't think so, madam. You must be mistaken.'

'Yes, I do. You're my Uncle Harry's brother, aren't you?'

'Harry who? I've never heard of him, who the hell are you – Interpol?' he asked.

'Interpol? No, I'm Eunice... Eunice Gayson. Or should I say Sargaison. I'm here making a film.'

His expression suddenly became very serious. In fact, his whole manner changed and he threatened to turf us all out into the pouring rain. Wondering what the hell was happening, Terence leapt off the wooden bench, holding his wallet up.

'*Are* you my Uncle Willy?' I asked. The man shuffled a little, and dismissed me with his hand. 'Look, I won't say a word to anyone, that I can promise you,' I added.

He looked at me, paused, and then asked how the hell I'd found him. Can you believe it – he *was* my Uncle Willy!

Although he was a little cagey about things, it turned out that he became the black sheep of his family by absconding to New

York with a chunk of the family fortune. He had his reasons, he said, but I didn't feel it wise to ask too much. While in America he'd lived the life of Reilly, blowing everything on wine, women and song – literally! When he thought he'd been spotted by the authorities he fled to the remoteness of North Africa. He'd obviously spent his fortune by now and was down on his luck, but at no point did he seem at all remorseful or sorry for his actions.

I would have said 'Let's keep in touch' but I doubt that would have gone down very well. Suffice to say he offered us what refreshments and warmth he had, and was pleasant company for a while. I kept my promise, and never spoke of him or our meeting... until now.

The weather cleared, we moved on, captured our footage and then made the journey back. I don't think Liz Taylor ever requested to join us on location again. Well, who could blame her?

Cut! Cut!

Towards the end of our location shoot in Morocco we were setting up for a scene involving yours truly being attacked by a ruthless assassin only to be saved by a soldier. It looked simple enough on paper, or so I thought.

Terence had asked the Commandant of the Spanish Foreign Legion, who were supplying the film with all the magnificent horses and riders, to pick one of his officers who could understand English to play the soldier. It was a small part with no dialogue, but as knives were involved he needed to understand the screen directions given. I was then introduced to a very charming young officer who had actually been educated in England and had no accent to speak of. 'Absolutely perfect,' I thought.

Terence took him to one side. 'Now listen carefully, I want you to follow my instructions *exactly*. When Miss Gayson is attacked, you rush in grab the knife and grapple the assailant to the ground, understand?'

Joining the Ranks

The young officer nodded in agreement. 'Any questions?' Terence asked. 'No, I understand,' he replied.

Terence shouted 'Action!' The knife-wielding assassin grabbed me, the soldier rushed in, took the knife and wrestled him to the ground.

'Cut! Cut!' Terence shouted, and turned to his cameraman to ask if everything was OK.

Now, you have to remember that Terence told the soldier to carry out his instructions exactly. So what did he do? He 'Cut!' my arm with the knife. Of course that particular shot isn't in the final film but I've still got the scar to prove it.

Zarak opened in New York on 26 December 1956. It did reasonable business and the young actor named Patrick McGoohan, so hotly tipped for success by Margaret Hinxman, did indeed go on to become a big star. In fact, the next time I saw him was when I played a guest role in his own television series, *Danger Man*, five years later.

Chapter Five

The Strange Case of Howard Hughes

With my work on *Zarak* complete, I returned to London thinking the break may have done our marriage some good, but things started going downhill from the moment I walked through the door. Leigh accused me of having affairs left right and centre while out in Morocco. I told him over and over that I was a one-man woman but he would never believe me. I felt helpless, lethargic, and quite hopeless. I slumped into a chair and sobbed, while he just stormed out.

I asked our housekeeper, who had heard everything, if she thought Leigh would ever change. She didn't quite know what to say, and just shook her head slightly and mumbled 'No.'

That was the last straw. I called my mother and sister, who, though fond of Leigh, convinced me to leave when they realised how he was treating me. 'This needs to be resolved now,' Pat said. 'You can't let it go on any longer.' I sat down and wrote Leigh a very honest and loving letter as to why I was leaving him. My hands were shaking and the tears were streaming down my cheeks as I poured my heart out, but I knew there was no going back. I packed a bag and walked out into the street, quite honestly not knowing what to do next. I returned home to my mother's and eventually moved into my own 'bachelor pad' in Mayfair.

Although we separated in 1956, Leigh never really wanted to accept that it was over, and he refused to divorce me at first. He even spoke to the *Daily Express* and hinted at a reconciliation at one point. The simple fact of the matter was that I wasn't his little baby any more and it took him a long time to realise that. We finally divorced in 1957, but despite all our problems we still remained friends.

Whenever I bumped into Leigh or met him for dinner – strictly as friends, I must add – he always broached the subject of getting back together, saying he still loved me. I laughed it off and changed the subject, but time after time he'd say it and in the end I told him, 'Friends is all we can ever be, and if you refuse to accept that then we can't see each other again.' He reluctantly agreed.

He later remarried but obviously nothing had changed, as his second wife eventually left him when his possessiveness and jealousy became too much for her to handle.

I was so pleased when Leigh's career as a writer and film producer really took off. He became highly respected in the business after founding the British Writers' Guild and becoming President of the International Writers' Guild. Then in the 1960s and early '70s he made 20 movies, including *The Black Windmill*, *The Frightened City* and *The Shakedown*. He moved out to Hollywood in the mid '70s and wrote for and produced several TV series.

On 5 October 1994 I received a phone call telling me that Leigh had died in Los Angeles after a brief illness. Though our life together was so much a thing of the past, the news still upset me. Despite everything that was said and done, I knew Leigh loved me. It was just a form of love I couldn't cope with.

I do the jokes

After splitting with Leigh I threw myself into work, and first up was *Alfred Marks Time*. In 1955 Independent Television (ITV) had been launched in the UK as the main competitor to the BBC, and the following year they premiered the first series of Alfred's hour-long sketch show, which became hugely popular and ran for four years. Katherine (Katie) Boyle, Bryan Johnson, Alan Wheatley and Michael Howard appeared with little old me in a series of parodies and revue-like routines, including an operatic duet with Alfred. Alfred's beautiful bass singing voice resulted in ITV receiving dozens of calls from viewers complementing whoever had actually sung the duet over the actor's lip movements! They assumed we'd been dubbed!

I'd acted with Alfred before in a musical called *The Kid from Stratford*. In this we had worked alongside one of Britain's top-rated comedians, Arthur Askey. He might have put across a nice, cheeky chappie persona on screen but he was notoriously difficult to work with, as he liked to be the sole centre of attention. During rehearsals Alfred and I would usually end up in absolute stitches, laughing and joking, which displeased Askey immensely. We'd often hear him muttering, 'Who the hell does he think he is? I'm the comedian around here,' which in turn made Alfred goad him even more.

I'll never forget the opening night in Manchester. Alfred and I had this big duet called 'The Promise in Your Eyes' and I thought the performance would be enhanced if I came on with some beautiful false eyelashes. I'd never worn them before but followed the instructions exactly; however, I must have used a little more glue than was required as one eye clamped shut! I was in a real panic. There was no time to do anything as I was due on stage within minutes. I had no choice but to walk on and Alfred, noticing my eye, decided it would be funny if he closed his – but the opposite one to mine. As you can imagine, it brought the house down, much to the annoyance of Arthur Askey, who had been well and truly upstaged. We could hardly sing for laughing but we soon realised, by the furious look on Askey's face, that we might be collecting our P45s on the way out.

Sure enough, the next day we were summoned to his dressing room for a real telling-off. I tried to explain, but he was having none of it and suggested we did it on purpose. Whatever I said Askey simply wouldn't listen and fired us both. I was in floods of tears as I thought, 'That's it, my career's over.' Alfred comforted me and said, 'Not to worry. We both hated that song anyway so perhaps Askey has done us a favour.'

Anyway, ITV came calling, not just for *Alfred Marks Time*, but also with an invitation to host *Palais Party*, which was to be broadcast live from the Hammersmith Palais every Friday night. Lou Preager (who also wrote and produced the show) appeared with his orchestra and vocalists Tina Vaughan and Steve Martin. In the first show 36 singers took part in a 'Find a Singer' competition – a bit of a forerunner of *The X-Factor* you might say. The show ran from June to September, and because it was only a one-nighter each week I was left free to pursue some radio work.

In fact, radio had been a staple part of my career since the 1940s, with the odd day here and there on BBC productions. I even hosted my own show on their competitor Radio Luxembourg, a show called, appropriately enough, *The Lady from Luxembourg*. I told my agent I was free to accept more offers. I loved radio; there was no need to get made up, wear fancy costumes or even learn long scripts.

Chaplin

Towards the end of the run of *Palais Party* I was offered a play. Producer Michael Argy was bringing over to the UK the Broadway hit *Oh Men! Oh Women!* and it was to open at the Pigalle in Liverpool before touring. I read the script, found it intriguing and asked who I would be playing opposite, but they wouldn't say. My agent, Al Parker, said he'd heard it was Sydney Chaplin, the elder half-brother of Charlie. I didn't quite see him in the part, as from what I'd read of the script it was a much younger character, but I thought it would be fun to work with a Chaplin.

After I signed on the dotted line, the producers called me up and asked if they could come down to the Hammersmith Palais, where I was rehearsing, to see me, adding, 'We'll introduce you to Charlie.'

I said, 'Don't you mean Sydney?'

'No, it's Charlie Chaplin Jr,' they replied.

I thought, 'Well, that could be even more interesting.' When he walked into my dressing room it was really quite strange; he had the same facial expressions and body movements as his famous father. Talk about a carbon copy. We got on very well, and all seemed set for success.

Before starting rehearsals the producer said, 'There's just one little matter I wanted to discuss with you... Charlie has a big drink problem, and I was hoping you might keep an eye on him.'

My heart sank; I didn't want that responsibility. 'If his drinking is going to be a problem then I'd really rather not do the play,' I told him.

'Oh, but he's on the wagon at the moment,' he reasoned.

I was a little apprehensive, but my agent said to give it a go and see how we got on during rehearsals. Well, Charlie didn't show any signs of being an alcoholic at all and was absolutely brilliant. I called my agent up and said, 'This is great. He's such a joy to be around and so professional.'

On the opening night in Liverpool, the producers, seeing how well we worked together, decided there and then to capitalise on our success, and indeed the earlier Broadway success, and announced that they were going to find a sponsor to bring us into the West End.

However, the second night was a different story. Charlie was smashed out of his mind; he couldn't remember the lines, he was all over the stage and I was terrified. Dealing with a drunken co-star live on stage isn't any fun, and this American comedy was one where I had to really be on the ball without any distractions.

Afterwards, I roasted Charlie. I asked how he could do this to himself, to me and to everyone else involved. I tried everything I knew to reason with him but by now he was so drunk that he was trying to fly out of the hotel window! I had to spend the night in his room watching him, and ended up talking to him about his troubled childhood, his estrangement from his father, being raised by his mother alone after his parents bitterly divorced, and so on. I was now not only his co-star, but his babysitter and analyst too.

I said to the producer the next morning, 'I can't go on, it's going to kill me.' I dreaded the next night, but – sod's law – Charlie was brilliant again. Word perfect. Then the worst possible thing happened a few nights later. Just as Charlie was getting into his stride, the great Charles Chaplin (Sr) came to see the play.

Afterwards he came backstage and said he thought I was fabulous and much better than the girl playing it in New York, etc etc. I cut in to ask if he'd seen Charlie Jr yet and he said 'No, not yet.' I said, 'He was absolutely wonderful tonight, wasn't he?' Chaplin didn't reply. Realising this was my chance to help my co-star I said, 'He needs to hear that from you, as he told me you never praised him for anything he's ever done, and that is why he drinks. He feels like a failure in your shadow.'

Charlie Chaplin Sr feigned a smile and left my dressing room. He didn't go round to see his son, though, and never once praised the wonderful performance he'd given that night. Thereafter Charlie Jr started to drink and drink and drink. I was becoming a nervous wreck and eventually they had to take the play off. It taught me a big lesson – never work with an actor who has a drink problem. Sadly Charlie Jr died in 1968, aged just 43.

Hollywood calling

As I mentioned, *Zarak* premiered in December 1956, around the time *Oh Men! Oh Women!* was on its short-lived tour. We were up in Edinburgh when one of the big American magazines ran a double-page feature on 'the most beautiful English actresses' and included a photograph of me!

The next thing I knew an American guy came backstage and said, 'Miss Gayson, I'd just like to say how much I enjoyed your performance tonight.' Luckily it was a night when Charlie was sober for most of the show, and he went on, 'I'm here on behalf of Mr Howard Hughes, have you ever heard of him?'

Not knowing if it was a wind-up or not, I thought I'd better play along. I said, 'Howard Hughes? Of course I've heard of him.' I mean, Hughes was a hugely famous filmmaker, owner of RKO Pictures, famed aviator and boss of Trans World Airlines just for starters! This chap produced the magazine article and went on, 'Mr Hughes saw this and wants to meet you.'

'OK, OK. Is this a wind up?' I asked.

He said, 'Would you have your agent ring this Hollywood number?'

Well, I knew the play was on the verge of folding, so I thought, 'What the hell, let's make the phone call.' I asked Al Parker to call and sure enough he came back to me and said Howard Hughes wanted me to fly to LA.

'Yes, but why me?' I asked.

'He said he has a particular part in a film he wants to discuss with you,' Al replied.

'Do I really want to go to meet Howard Hughes?' I asked.

'If you want to be a millionaire in the next year or so, then why not?'

I flew out on TWA, naturally, and boy did they look after me. I had a private section in the plane all to myself, which was absolutely ridiculous. They waited on me hand and foot and ensured that my every whim was attended to. Once we landed, I was escorted down the stairs of the plane ahead of all the other passengers, and across the tarmac to a huge black Cadillac where three 'hoods' were waiting.

The Strange Case of Howard Hughes

'Miss Gayson, follow us.'

'Who are you and where are we going?'

They said they were from the Hughes office. The people on the plane were all looking out of the windows and no doubt thinking 'Who the hell is she?' Anyhow, I was taken to Chateau Marmont – a big block of apartments on Sunset Boulevard – and straight up to the penthouse. 'This is yours while in Hollywood,' they said, 'but there's no time to lose, we have to go downtown.'

I was then taken to a photographic studio on Sunset Boulevard and thought, 'Come on, I've just crossed the Atlantic and I'm worn out. They aren't going to take pictures of me looking like this?' We went into a back room and another man from the Hughes office told me, 'Mr Hughes will be with you directly,' before offering me coffee.

I waited... and waited... and waited. An hour later, feeling a bit miffed, I thought about booking a ticket back home when the door opened and in walked this rather emaciated man dressed in what looked like an all-in-one cotton suit, sporting long hair and a very bushy beard, with very long nails. But far from looking as he sounds, he was actually quite well-groomed; weird-looking but well-groomed.

'Good evening, Miss Gayson, I'm Howard Hughes and I've been looking forward to meeting you,' he said in a rather cultured voice.

'Why, is there a specific part you have in mind for me?'

'No, this is just a general meeting,' he said.

Having heard Anita Ekberg talk about RKO, I really hoped I wasn't going to be one of those people who was signed up and then disappeared from the industry, as nearly happened to her, and indeed as nearly happened to me at Rank.

'I've heard very good reviews of your latest play and your performance in it,' he said, before switching subjects totally to talk about philosophy for what seemed like hours. After the long flight

I was absolutely exhausted and just had to interrupt him.

'Do forgive me but I am very tired, it was a very long journey and I've just finished a play...'

'OK,' he said. 'It's been very interesting talking to you. You'll be seeing me again and thank you once more for coming. I'm going to assign my people and their wives to be with you, very nice people.'

I asked, 'Do you mean the Mormons you sponsor?'

'How do you know about them?' he asked.

'Well, I read that your plane crashed in the desert and you were rescued by the Mormons, and you built the first Mormon church and have financed them ever since.'

Impressed by my knowledge of him, he said, 'I'd like you to meet *your* team.' He introduced me to a very well-attired woman who was to be my personal secretary for the duration of my stay. She explained that I could go anywhere I wanted, though I had to be accompanied by her at all times as 'Mr Hughes likes you to be looked after.'

She added, 'I'm staying in the penthouse apartment with you; if that's all right, of course? I can stay in my own apartment if you wish, but it's usual for me to stay with you.'

I thought this was getting weirder and declined her offer to stay. I returned to the apartment and picked up the phone to ring my agent. I just didn't feel at ease. I couldn't get an outside line so I rang the concierge, who said I couldn't dial out and to wait for my secretary the next morning!

Dog tired, I went to bed and slept. The secretary turned up at ten o'clock the next morning and said, 'Now we're going shopping.' I asked what for and she replied, 'Jewels, furs, clothes, whatever you want.'

'But I have all my clothes I want to wear here with me; I'm not going to be here that long... Am I?"

She went 'Well...' and laughed.

'Why can't I use the phone?' I asked.

She wouldn't answer. I asked her again and she said she had no information on that.

I needed to get out, so I agreed to go shopping. She pointed out various dresses, which I refused. Then she said, 'Do you mind if I buy them and put them down on your expenses?' So she bought all these clothes and I came away with one pair of shoes. She then took me to a hotel in Beverly Hills for lunch and over the other side of the restaurant I spotted Hazel Court, whom I knew; she waved and said 'Eunice, hi, how are you?'

The secretary was immediately on the case and asked 'Do you know her?' 'Yes,' I said, 'she's an English actress.'

When I asked Hazel to join us, the secretary snapped, 'Sorry, no. Mr Hughes wouldn't like it.'

'Mr Hughes wouldn't like it?' I queried.

'Look, you must accept what I'm saying. I don't want to lose my job and if you go over to her or she comes over to you, Mr Hughes really wouldn't like that.'

Perplexed, I called over to Hazel, 'Give your number to the waiter and I'll call you.' Fat chance of that; little did I know that, not only couldn't I make phone calls out, but no one could ring in either!

If I so much as said 'Hello' to anyone the secretary was straight on my case. 'Do you know her? Do you know him?' Hughes, meanwhile, wanted me to sign a long-term contract with RKO. 'A contract to do what exactly?' I asked. Of course, I never got a straight answer; they just went on about how Mr Hughes liked me and wanted to make me a big star in the USA.

'Yeah, yeah, yeah,' I thought. He'd said that to Anita Ekberg and goodness knows how many others too.

Their thinking was obviously to keep me busy, as I had photographic sessions booked until they were coming out of my ears. Then there were more blessed shopping trips with the secretary and it was all fast becoming a nightmare. I did everything but audition for a film role – which, as far as I was concerned, was my only reason for being there.

Back at Chateau Marmont, I had the bright idea of saying I needed to speak to my agent about the contract, and asked if they could get him on the phone, to which they agreed as long as the secretary was present. Al Parker's assistant, Richard, came on the line very excitedly saying he'd had a huge offer from Howard Hughes. I asked, 'What *exactly* is it for?'

'What do you care?' he replied. 'You'll be rich!'

'All you care about is your ten per cent. I'm a working actress. How is this going to further my career? I can't live, being locked up with all these restrictions they impose on me!'

The secretary gave me the evil eye and I realised I'd overstepped the mark with my rather blunt conversation. 'Well, the decision is yours,' Richard said, 'but I think you're nuts, you'll be a millionaire in about 18 months.' And he rang off. Just as I was about to put the receiver down, I heard a click. They'd obviously been listening in. The secretary gave me strict instructions that I should be ready at 9:00 am the next morning for, yes, you guessed it, another shopping trip, then left the apartment.

No one understood how bad the situation was; how could they? Well, the maid did actually – she was English – and she could see just how concerned and desperate I was becoming. In a quiet moment she offered to help, saying that she couldn't get me past Hughes' men in the hallway but there was another option – the laundry chute!

'The laundry chute?' I exclaimed.

'Yes,' she replied. 'You're slim enough to fit in it and I'll make sure it's a soft landing. There's a drug store opposite, Schwab's, where you can make a call. Do you know anyone in LA?'

I immediately thought of Charlie, a friend who now lived there. I was sure he'd help.

The Strange Case of Howard Hughes

So I made good my escape, zooming down the chute with soiled linen, and after a few hairy moments I found myself in the basement. The maid helped me up and out of a side door where I ran across to the drug store. However, before I could finish my telephone conversation Hughes' men arrived to escort me back to Chateau Marmont.

They knew I was trouble. Next thing my so-called secretary was told by one of Mr Hughes' staff that I should be 'taken away and given time to think, as I really wasn't fitting in very well with the Hughes regime.'

It sounded quite threatening, and rather final to my mind. But my secretary then adopted a far more genteel manner than I'd been used to.

'What would you like to do, Miss Gayson?' she asked. 'Maybe a change of scenery would help you relax. How about Mexico?'

Thinking on my feet, I said, 'No, I'd like to go and visit my Aunt Eunice. She has a suite at the Pierre Hotel in New York. But of course Mr Hughes wouldn't like that, would he?'

'What a great idea!' she enthused.

I wasn't sure what tactics they were now employing, but they did allow me to go to New York and see my aunt, and of course I told her the full story. She said we should call the police, but I asked her not to. I just wanted to get away from Hughes, and someone as powerful and influential as him would probably have the police in his pocket. She then had the idea of flying to Barbados.

'I'll book a flight and we can stay at the Bermudiana,' she told me. The Bermudiana Hotel was owned by Miriam Weston, who was married to Garfield Weston of Weston's Biscuits and was a great friend of mine from London.

Knowing we were being watched, Aunt Eunice had a word with the hotel manager to see if we could get out of a side door without anyone knowing. He suggested a disused back door, outside which we could pick up a yellow cab. All went swimmingly until we reached the airport. When we went to collect our tickets we noticed we were flying with TWA. But we hadn't booked TWA!

We landed in Barbados and I noticed on a news-stand the headline 'Hughes...' Then, meeting our friends at the airport, they said the hotel was really busy as 'Howard Hughes and his entourage have just taken the whole top floor.' I thought, 'I'll never get rid of this man!'

My aunt was terrified. I said, 'The only way to escape him will be if I board a flight back to London here and now.' So I did. Amazingly I wasn't stopped, though my heart was in my mouth every step of the way to the departure gate. I landed back in London, so relieved and so exhausted. I looked around nervously for 'hoods' at the airport and in cars outside, but there was nobody and nothing from the Hughes organisation. From that day to this I never heard from him or his entourage ever again. Looking back, I guess I was really quite lucky to have met Hughes – many tried, very few succeeded.

Anyway, on my arrival home, my first task was to change agents. Al Parker wouldn't be getting any more commission out of me!

Taking a dip

Carry On Admiral was not one of the popular Peter Rogers comedy films; in fact, it pre-dated that series by a year. No, this was a comic tale from writer/director Val Guest, whom I'd previously worked with on *Dance Little Lady*. David Tomlinson, Peggy Cummins, Joan Sims, A E Matthews, Ronald Shiner and many more beloved British film stars headed the cast. I played Jane Godfrey (Matthews' daughter). It was a comedy based on two friends getting drunk and switching identities; one is a public relations executive, whereas the other is captain of a ship.

In one quite alarming incident I was to be knocked overboard by the wash of a boat and Val Guest said, 'You can swim, can't you?'

I said, 'Yes' ... but I would be fully clothed... 'which is slightly different. And what about the undercurrent?'

'Oh, don't worry about that. We'll have rescue boats and a swimmer standing by. Would that make you happy?'

I said, 'Yes, OK.'

Now, Portsmouth harbour (where we were filming) is treacherous. Its strong currents are well known and the wash knocking me over was from quite a big ship, so I'd be going in with some force. The boat came round and the wash was terrific. I flew into the air and hit the water at a rate of knots and went down like a lead balloon. After a bit of a panic and a lot of arm waving, I finally made it up and got a gulp of air before being hit again by the wash! Down I went; this kept happening, and being fully clothed I wasn't at my most buoyant. It was absolutely terrifying. I really thought 'This is it.'

Finally a hand reached out and grabbed me, pulled me up and into the camera boat. Val was there and said, 'That was fabulous, sweetheart. It really looked as if you were drowning!'

How right he was. What's more, Val later admitted the professional swimmer had refused to do it, thinking it too dangerous!

The awful thing is, when I went to see the film I saw the wash coming and me going over, then they cut to another scene. Talk about nearly dying for your art!

In my next little film, *Light Fingers*, I was cast in the lead role of Rose Levenham, a woman who can't resist auctions. Her husband Humphrey (Roland Culver) convinces himself that she's a kleptomaniac and hires a private detective (Guy Rolfe) to keep an eye on her. Meanwhile, Rose realises that the watchdog is himself a thief, trying to frame her for items *he* stole. I'm afraid the film didn't set the world on fire, though it did give skiffle king Lonnie Donegan his big break as a film composer.

It was then back to the theatre, and back to *Born Yesterday* at Richmond Theatre, no less! Not co-starring with Hartley Power this time, but with Robert Beatty. I thought he was very good in the part but perhaps just a little too refined. Anyhow, what does it matter as on stage he was fantastic, and we subsequently went on a tour which was judged a huge success. Everyone said it was a better production than the West End version!

Then I reported back to the BBC for *What the Doctor Ordered*, a lovely 90-minute TV farce, starring Leo Franklyn, Brian Rix, Hazel Douglas and little old me as a gold-digging girlfriend. The story centred on Lord J G Van Velt (Franklyn), who was the owner of a large casket of pills, all with different uses; the one he was interested in was the rejuvenation pill, but the labels had come off and it became a case of trial and error.

It's odd that I should round off 1957 with medical matters, as another doctor was waiting to enter my life at the beginning of 1958 – though this one was more interested in body parts than rejuvenation pills!

Chapter Six

An Appointment with Hammer

One of the regular directors of the *Douglas Fairbanks Presents* series was Terence Fisher, who most famously went on to direct some of the very best Hammer horror films. My association with Hammer, if you recall, went back to 1950 with *To Have and To Hold*. Well, here is where it all starts knitting together in one of those very happy chains of events...

In 1956 Terence Fisher directed me as Elizabeth Anders in a film called *The Last Man To Hang?* Tom Conway, Elizabeth Sellars and Anthony Newley were also in the cast, and I remember it being a very dramatic script set around a murder trial. Tom Conway's character (Sir Roderick Strood) had supposedly poisoned his wife (Sellars) and, with the 1950s' parliamentary attempt to abolish the death penalty in full focus, it was heady stuff. Damning evidence was provided by Strood's former housekeeper, Mrs Tucker (Freda Jackson), who would do anything to see her ex-employer swinging from a gibbet. If found guilty he would surely hang. Fortunately, Strood was found not guilty, which was just as well as his supposedly dead wife turned out to be very much alive! It was all a ploy to get rid of him, devised with the help of a young charmer called Cyril Gaskin (Newley).

Tom Conway, by the way, was George Sanders' brother, and sounded just like him; if I closed my eyes on set I could have sworn it was George delivering the lines. As for Anthony Newley, he was a fast-rising star at the time and I was really surprised how big-headed he'd suddenly become. I'd met him a couple of times, with and without his then wife Joan Collins, and he'd always come across as being a charming, down to earth and very polite gentleman. Now, the reverse was true; he was very loud, arrogant, and threw his weight around all the time. Why? I have no idea.

A true professional

Anyway, I greatly enjoyed working with Terence Fisher, and around 18 months later he came back into my life following a big Variety Club fundraising event in London where I'd been introduced to Peter Cushing. As with most actors, our conversation drifted to recent projects and I mentioned that I'd worked, very happily, with Terence Fisher. Peter's eyes widened.

'Have you ever been offered a Hammer horror?' he asked.

'No, no one has ever asked me,' I replied.

'Well, I'm asking you! There's one coming up in which you would be absolutely perfect for a role, and Terence is directing.'

Hammer had by then reinvented itself as a successful horror production company with *The Quatermass Xperiment*, *The Curse of Frankenstein* and *Dracula*; next up was *The Revenge of Frankenstein*. Peter sent me his own personal copy of the script, which I read before being invited to a meeting, after which they offered me the role of Margaret Conrad, a voluntary worker at Dr Stein's home for the needy. (In reality, the reinvented Baron Frankenstein's cover in order to obtain a regular supply of the body parts he needed to carry out his ghoulish experiments.) I joined a cast which included Peter, Francis Matthews, Lionel Jeffries and Michael Gwynn.

Being amidst the buzz and exciting atmosphere on a Hammer production at Bray Studios was quite a thrill. Don't get me wrong, the budgets weren't huge and time was tight, but they knew how to use every last penny to make the sets and costumes look like they'd cost a million dollars.

Working with the wonderful Peter Cushing was a joy; he was so kind, so gentle and so giving with fellow actors. He was totally, totally unlike the crazed and warped characters he so often played, and was adored by everybody both in front of and behind the cameras. On my first day he made a point of saying 'Welcome to the family.' Every day thereafter, when I arrived on set in the morning, he'd be waiting to greet me, kissing my hand, and would be concerned about how I'd slept and whether I needed anything before we started shooting. He was never afraid to pay any kind of compliment and if he thought you looked beautiful he'd tell you. Believe me, those kind of comments from a leading man are a real rarity in this business. I remember he once said to me, 'If there is anything in the script you don't like or think could be improved, we'll change it. Just say.'

We may have changed the odd word here and there, but nothing major. Peter always took on board what anyone said though, be it about a camera position or a light, and suggested it quietly to the director to see if indeed it could be improved. I can honestly say I've never heard a bad word said about Peter. He was a true professional, never drying or fluffing a single line.

Horsing around

However, another co-star proved very temperamental and troublesome to me – a four-legged co-star, I should add. In one particular scene I was to ride across a courtyard on horseback; simple enough, or so I thought. I'd never ridden a horse in my life and was a little uneasy at the prospect, so to boost my confidence the company sent me down to stables near Hyde Park to be introduced to the horse they were using in the film. He seemed friendly, and I trotted around a little, enough to get away with acting as though I knew what I was doing.

Back at Bray, the day arrived to shoot the courtyard scene. I was now in full Victorian riding garb, which was incredibly heavy but looked magnificent. The plan was to make sure the horse would get used to the weight so it wouldn't cause any problems during the scene. Well, that was the plan. I climbed on the horse and he bucked. The trainer calmed him down and explained it was just an initial reaction to the weight and lights, one of which had just fallen over, and assured me that everything would be fine. I believed him.

It was a very mild winter's day, and sitting around on horseback on the stage, with the heat of the lights coupled with my large costume, waistcoat, top hat and cloak, made me feel so very hot. There was some slight delay which kept us waiting, when, suddenly, my four-legged friend reared. My left foot came out of the stirrup and I fell to the floor.

I'd twisted my ankle quite badly, or at least I thought so. The unit nurse came over, fussing, and wanted to apply a support bandage. Terence was concerned, not only for me, but also about continuity in finishing the scene. I said, 'Look, the Victorians are very straight and stiff and my dress goes right down over my ankle. The bandage will be fine and out of sight.'

Though in some pain, I carried on and got through the scene. Well, the show must go on and all that. Only afterwards, after being taken for an X-ray, did I discover that I'd actually broken my ankle! Luckily I'd finished shooting by then. The doctor was amazed at my seemingly high pain threshold; we Gaysons are obviously made of tough stuff! And, after taking a nice few weeks' break with my mother in Brighton (who, incidentally, couldn't believe I'd broken my ankle on set and just carried on shooting), it was straight back to work, albeit with a bit of a limp for several weeks.

As is so common in this industry, you finish a film and move on to the next job, not knowing when you might see your co-stars again. Well, after this film the only time I ever met Peter Cushing again was at the very same Variety Club fundraiser a year later. We both joked that we could only stand seeing each other once a year; Peter had a terrific sense of humour. I'm only sorry I didn't have the chance of working with him again.

The film, incidentally, was released as part of a double-bill in the USA with *Curse of the Demon*, starring my friend Peggy Cummins. Together again on the big screen... well, sort of!

'Exotic' locations

Around this time, various TV engagements continued to come my way. *The New Adventures of Charlie Chan* was a crime drama series made in 1957; the first five episodes were made in the United States before production switched to the United Kingdom under Lew Grade's ITC Entertainment banner. The series followed the investigations of the fictional detective Chan and I appeared in episode 28, *The Hands of Hera Dass*. American actor J Carrol Naish played Chan, and my rather forgettable episode was only notable for having been directed by Leslie Arliss.

Afterwards I appeared in the *This Hungry Hell* episode of another TV drama series, *White Hunter*, with Christopher Lee as my fellow guest star. This one was set entirely in the big game reserves of Africa. 'Great,' I thought, 'a big location and a nice holiday in the sun.'

Hmm. If only. It was actually shot at Beaconsfield Studios. American actor Rhodes Reason was shipped over to play Hunter and all the African location sequences were obtained by using scratchy old stock footage!

Needless to say, when my agent then called and asked if I wanted a guest part in a Caribbean adventure show, set on board a 100-foot boat, I asked where would we be filming, Tilbury Docks? I wasn't far off! The 30-minute episodes of *Adventures of the Sea Hawk* starred John Howard, and once again no expense was lavished.

The BBC subsequently invited me to play Lady Fanny Kostaki in *Educated Evans* opposite Charlie Chester. It was a TV remake of a Max Miller comedy film from the 1930s, set in the world of horse racing, where a hapless tipster is given the job of training a prize horse by the two equally hapless social climbers who bought it. Hot on the heels of *Evans*, the Beeb kindly offered me an episode of the drama series *Duty Bound* with Dermot Walsh, followed by *Make Mine Music*, produced by John Street. Then the other side, ITV, asked me to join the guest panel of *I've Got a Secret* with Jon Pertwee, Sid James and Sarah Leighton. This was the first of a new Wednesday night series modelled on *What's My Line?* It was all good exposure, I thought.

On thin ice

Sonja Henie, when aged just 14, became the Norwegian Skating Champion, and at 15 she won the first of three Olympic gold medals.

In 1936 she turned professional and was touring with her own ice show when 20th Century-Fox signed her and she debuted in *One in a Million*, in which she played – guess what? – an ice skater. The picture was very successful and Sonja continued to make movies throughout the late 1930s and early '40s. I think it would be fair to say the films were more a testament to her skating skills than her acting ability.

In 1958, she decided to try her luck in the UK. *Hello London* was a semi-documentary film following her arrival in London, through to her performing at various ice shows. It was absolutely littered with guest appearances from Michael Wilding, Dora Bryan, Roy Castle, Dennis Price, Stanley Holloway... and me, all playing ourselves. There was also a young actor who played a photographer; he was making his film debut. His name? Oliver Reed.

I'm afraid Sonja was a complete so-and-so to me and Michael Wilding. There was nothing we could do about it. Her husband was a multi-millionaire and was financing the movie, while she was producing it – which she made known in no uncertain terms. I said to Michael, 'Let's just enjoy it and have a laugh.' He said, 'I can't, but you must, otherwise it's going to be hell.'

Sonja used to watch rehearsals and I said to Michael, 'Did you see that little head poking around the door? Our routine is going to be axed.' He said, 'No, I love it, it's the best thing we've done in the film.' But, sure enough, the next day Sonja said, 'My husband and I felt your routine didn't fit in with the overall feel of the scene.' In fact, it would have simply upstaged her; that was the only reason she cut it.

She even had the audacity to say to me one day, 'I adore you, Eunice, but the trouble with you is that you're too damn talented,' obviously hoping I'd swoon after her like the other people she surrounded herself with. Oh no, I had her number. Poor Michael was a nervous wreck by the end of it, as Sonja cut virtually everything we did together. Our biggest number was left as background with her in front of it doing a twee ice-skating routine.

She had very little sense of humour, which drove us up the wall. We always tried to make it all fun while she hated to think we were having any sort of enjoyment at her expense. Bizarrely, almost as though she'd been unaware of her terrible attitude towards us 'lesser stars', at the end of the film she gave me a lovely diamond brooch and said how lovely it was working with me. I thought, 'What?' Unfortunately, the brooch was stolen on the set of another film and when Michael Wilding heard he said, 'Oh, she got it back!' I said, 'Don't be so naughty,' but almost believed it!

Personalities aside, Sonja was a very astute businesswoman. Such was her financial acumen that she was one of the ten wealthiest women in the world when she died in 1969.

Tea and cake

While enjoying film and TV work, I loved theatre tremendously, so when Emile Littler contacted me, saying he was bringing an old

Frederick Lonsdale comedy to the London stage, I was intrigued. This one had never been seen in the West End before, but had played on Broadway as *Once is Enough* in 1938 and 20 years later as *Half a Loaf* at the Theatre Royal, Windsor. Now it was retitled *Let Them Eat Cake* and opened at the Cambridge Theatre in the West End on 6 May 1959.

'12 Stars' read the billboard over the theatre entrance, and the cast was certainly impressive, including Michael Denison, Dulcie Gray, James Sharkey (who later became a big theatrical agent), Guy Middleton, Claude Hulbert, Henry Kendall, Phyllis Neilson-Terry, Austin Melford and Jean Lodge. Oh, and me – as Liz Pleydell. Set in 1913, it was a typical Lonsdale comedy of manners, with no fewer than eight of the characters being Lords, Ladies, Dukes or Duchesses. It was such a joyous production, with wonderful reviews. I loved Michael and Dulcie dearly, and being on stage with them was an absolute pleasure.

As the 1950s drew to a close, I wondered what might come up next. Little did I realise I was about to move into the busiest period of my career.

My first stage appearance of the new decade came in June 1960 with a production of *The Little Hut* for the Famous Players in Weston-super-Mare. I played the guest lead, Susan. We opened at the newly refurbished Playhouse and the local newspaper headline exclaimed, 'Eunice Gayson Attracts.' Attracts what, you might ask!

On the subject of attraction, you've probably realised by now that I'm not one to tittle-tattle about any romantic encounters I've had over the years – not that there were that many before I married Leigh. I'm essentially a private person, and very much a one-man woman, but there is one dalliance that is worthy of a mention.

Porfirio Rubirosa was a diplomat from the Dominican Republic, but his reputation as a Lothario and international playboy overshadowed his political work and certainly earned him more newspaper headlines. He was in fact regarded as one of the world's greatest lovers, having bedded such beauties as Zsa Zsa Gabor, and married wealthy American women, including Doris Duke and Woolworths' heiress Barbara Hutton. The latter, incidentally, funded his jet-set lifestyle, and also fuelled his passion for fast cars (and no doubt fast women too). He was married five times in all.

I'd heard he'd been interested in me for a while and, after a chance meeting with him at a party, when I was a young, free singleton, I thought 'What the hell, why not?' Boy oh boy, what a disappointment! It really was a case of a reputation preceding him, a reputation built on self-publicity and self-belief. I certainly, if you will pardon the expression, had my fill of him!

And then there was a certain John F Kennedy. His reputation similarly preceded him, but ... once bitten twice shy. So that was, thankfully, an encounter I managed to avoid!

Night of 100 Stars x 3

In July 1960, famed theatrical producers Lance Hamilton and Charles Russell asked if I would take part in a huge extravaganza entitled *Night of a Hundred Stars*, which aimed to raise much-needed funds for the Actors' Orphanage. It was to be held at the London Palladium and star, as you've probably guessed, one hundred of the biggest names from the world of music, film and theatre. And I mean *real* stars, the cream of the crop, not these reality show types we see nowadays who are famous just for being famous.

They didn't need to ask me twice. It was a hugely glamorous affair. I remember Laurence Olivier and Kenneth More being an absolute scream when they appeared dressed as two frightfully English ladies. Then dear Johnny Mills, in the guise of Charlie Chaplin, brought a lump to my throat in a wonderful mime sketch with his daughter Juliet, followed by Flora Robson belting out 'There is Nothing Like a Dame' backed by the unlikeliest chorus of George Baker, Alan Bates, Gordon Jackson, Leslie Phillips and Robert Beatty – that was a sight to behold.

The wonderful thing about this show was that no one was afraid to step out of their comfort zone and everyone was willing to do whatever was necessary for the worthy cause. So where does yours truly come into it? Peggy Cummins, Fenella Fielding, Miriam Karlin, Millicent Martin, Sheila Sim, Maggie Smith, Sylvia Syms and I had an absolute blast performing 'Keep Young and Beautiful', burlesque style. The whole evening was so much fun that we never stopped laughing from beginning to end and it all helped raise about £11,000.

They asked me back for another *Night* in 1963 and I was more than happy to return, as were my chums Peggy Cummins and Sylvia Syms. This time we were teamed up with Janette Scott, Anna Massey, Liz Fraser, Hayley Mills, Juliet Mills and Judi Dench to perform a brilliantly choreographed showgirl routine; it went down so well they invited us back for the next year's show.

Though when you look at the line-up of the previous ones it was hard to imagine how, in 1964, they could top them. But when Judy Garland was announced, that really was something! Garland wasn't expected to sing, we were told, but on the night she treated the audience to wonderful renditions of 'Over the Rainbow' and 'Swannee', receiving rapturous applause and, I must say, one of the longest standing ovations I've ever witnessed. I met Garland afterwards, but found her a little uptight. Maybe she was just nervous about performing on stage again, or perhaps unhappy with the shade of the red carpet that she (or her manager) had demanded be laid from her dressing room to the side of the stage. Who knows?

To top it, as if you could top Judy Garland, two final surprise guests appeared in the guise of Gloria Swanson and Merle Oberon. Backstage I'd decided Swanson certainly lived up to her name as she spent the entire evening swanning around as though she owned the place. Then again, she was Hollywood royalty so that was to be expected, I guess.

I, meanwhile, along with Jane Asher, Adrienne Corri, Wendy Craig, Peggy Cummins, Angela Douglas and Elisabeth Welch, performed a Black and White Minstrels routine with the wonderful Harry Secombe. (Of course, you wouldn't be able to get away with blacking-up these days.) Other stars who appeared on stage included Laurence Olivier, Frankie Vaughan, Dame Edith Evans and Beryl Reid, before Shirley Bassey, as always, blew the roof off the theatre by nailing a version of Noël Coward's 'I Believe'.

In an exhausted stupor, I bumped into the adorable Barbara Windsor on the way home. We both agreed that it was one of the most glamorous nights of our entire lives, made all the more satisfying by knowing we'd raised thousands for charity.

Chapter Seven

The Hills Are Alive...

Most people are familiar with the 1965 film version of *The Sound of Music* starring Julie Andrews and Christopher Plummer, but the original musical on which the film is based, written by Richard Rodgers and Oscar Hammerstein, began its life on Broadway back in 1959. The musical was itself based on a book by Howard Lindsay and Russel Crouse adapted from a true story, *The Trapp Family Singers*, by Maria Augusta Trapp.

The original stage version starred Mary Martin as Maria and Theodore Bikel as Captain Baron von Trapp – a widowed ex-naval officer with seven children who rules the family home with rigid order and discipline. But with the arrival of a new governess, Maria, things start to change for the better as she brings a breath of fresh air into the family, teaching the children to sing and to really enjoy 'the sound of music', through which she also melts Captain von Trapp's icy heart. He and Maria fall in love, but before they can do anything about it Austria comes under Nazi rule in 1938 and war looms on the horizon – a war in which the Captain will be forced to fight against his own country.

Rodgers and Hammerstein had already enjoyed major Broadway successes with *Oklahoma*, *Carousel*, *The King and I*, *State Fair* and *South Pacific* before they turned their talents to this project. *The Sound of Music* opened at the Lunt-Fontanne Theatre on Broadway on 16 November 1959. With fairly favourable reviews overall, and more importantly excellent word of mouth, the show became incredibly popular with theatregoers, running until mid-1963, clocking up 1443 performances, and receiving several accolades, not least tying with *Fiorello* for the 'Best Musical' Tony award. The cast album sold three million copies and a transfer to London's glittering West End was assured.

First encounters

I first met Oscar Hammerstein while visiting my dear Aunt Eunice in Scarsdale, New York. I must have been around 16 at the time and remember it being my first transatlantic trip – a huge adventure for a young girl like myself. Aunt Eunice was a close friend of the Hammersteins and one day took me along to meet Oscar and his wife Dorothy, who lived close to her house on Oak Lane. Oscar told me my aunt had the most incredible ear and she 'just knew' if something he had written would be a hit or not. He'd often call her up and say, 'Eunice, I've just written something. Can you pop over and lend me your ear?'

It was actually quite amazing as she'd never had any kind of musical training at all – it was all down to instinct. Thinking back, the whole experience was rather surreal. I'd just met one half of the most respected composing duo in the business and he gave me advice about pursuing a career in the theatre while telling me he relied on my aunt's untrained ear to determine if *he* would have a hit or not! How many people would have killed for that opportunity? Little did I know that, later, I would not only appear in one of Rodgers and Hammerstein's most successful shows, but that it would become a huge part of my life for many years.

Singing for my supper

Fast forward to the early 1960s. I was at a dinner party in London and was introduced to Richard Rodgers, Oscar's famous partner. Unbeknown to me he'd seen me in *Let Them Eat Cake* at the

Cambridge Theatre and, after complimenting me on my acting performance, said, 'It's a shame you can't sing.'

'Actually, I was trained as an opera singer!' I replied.

'Really?' he said.

'Yes, I really am a trained singer,' I affirmed.

He explained that, after the success of *The Sound of Music* on Broadway, they were planning the show's transfer to London and hadn't yet cast the role of Elsa Schraeder, the Baroness. Rodgers said he was travelling back to the United States the next morning but if I was interested he'd arrange a flight for me to New York to audition. How could I possibly refuse?

The very next day an accompanist arrived at my flat and proceeded to run through what would be required at the audition, and the following day a plane ticket to New York arrived. This guy was serious!

On the flight out I found myself sitting next to Roger Dann, who coincidentally was auditioning for the role of Captain George Von Trapp. Dann was a very well-known French actor who'd worked with Édith Piaf for many years and then found fame in Hollywood with Alfred Hitchcock's *I Confess* in 1953.

I auditioned for Richard Rodgers at the Schubert Theatre on West 44th Street. Sadly, Oscar had died shortly after the production had opened on Broadway. I only wish he'd been there so I could have told him about my Aunt Eunice introducing us years earlier. Anyway, Rodgers seemed rather pleased when I finished my piece, leapt up and declared I'd be perfect for the part – the role was mine if I wanted it. Without hesitation I accepted.

Flying back from New York was an absolute nightmare as American Airlines' staff had decided to go on strike and all transatlantic flights had been cancelled. Luckily, domestic flights weren't affected so I decided that, rather than try to head home, I'd call up my old friend Diana Dors in Hollywood to see if she was free. Thankfully she was and so I spent the next couple of weeks enjoying her company and all that Los Angeles had to offer.

There was quite a British contingent in LA, with whom Diana loved to socialise, including Roger Moore and James Mason, and she often went bowling with them – and invited me! This was around the time Roger was having, shall we say, 'difficulties' with his then wife Dorothy Squires. He often appeared at Diana's house just to escape and get a little peace and quiet away from her rather domineering ways.

The airline strike was duly settled and we returned to the UK. Diana was heading back to shoot a film and I needed to prepare for the impending West End rehearsals. Initially we were told that the show would be staged for a year – no more, no less. That was a relief, as indefinite runs make it virtually impossible to live any kind of normal life and, with regular TV and film work out of the question, it takes you off the radar of producers and casting directors.

On day one of rehearsals I met the rest of the cast. Jean Bayliss was playing Maria Rainer. She'd taken over from Julie Andrews in the role of Polly in *The Boy Friend* on Broadway in the mid-1950s and had even spent three months sleeping on Julie's sofa; now there's a coincidence. Olive Gilbert was cast as Sister Margaretta; Olive was a favourite of Ivor Novello and had performed in many of his great musicals. Also in the company were Constance Shacklock, a noted opera singer who year after year would appear at 'The Last Night of the Proms', belting out Rule Britannia to much acclaim, and Harold Kasket, a British actor who could usually be found playing Arabs or mid-European types in films and TV. And then there was my fellow traveller Roger Dann as Captain George Von Trapp.

Union trouble

Rehearsals consisted of long days; leaving the theatre before 10.00 pm was unheard of. It was a difficult show to stage with many 'technical things' going on in the background, and in that respect was quite advanced for its time.

The night before we opened was an absolute nightmare. It was our final dress rehearsal and every time someone started their big number, something always happened – the scenery didn't move as it should, the lights stopped working, or there were off-notes from the orchestra. You name it, it went wrong. Ten o'clock came and went and we were still rehearsing. Then one of the chorus members reminded everyone that she was the company's Equity representative.

'Excuse me,' she said. 'I just want to warn you that I'm putting in a full report to Equity about this and then I am going home.'

Everyone was aghast. We were more than happy to work the extra hours because we opened the next day and there was still a lot of work to be done. Our director, Jerry Whyte, looked puzzled.

'Who are you?' he asked.

'I am one of the singers in the chorus in case you haven't noticed,' she said.

'Oh yeah, I've noticed all right. If you walk out that door I'll make sure you never work on a production in this country again, got it?'

'Who do you think you're talking to? I've got Equity behind me!' she exclaimed.

'Isn't it extraordinary that the stars of the show aren't objecting and are only too pleased to carry on because we open tomorrow but *you*, the least of the pack, are creating!' Jerry snapped.

'I'm going home. Hands up those who are going to join me,' the trouble-maker said.

I held my breath. Curtain up was in less than 24 hours and if any of the nuns were to leave now, the opening would be totally jeopardised. Mercifully nobody put their hands up.

'Right, as Equity members you'll all be reported,' she said and then stormed off.

Jerry shouted 'Goodbye' after her and thanked us all for our loyalty. 'Come on, let's get this right,' he said.

We never heard from Equity, but in another hour or so we had it – that extra time was really worth investing. If that over-zealous union rep could have brought the whole production to a complete standstill she would have done.

Throughout the hectic rehearsal period Richard Rodgers continually assured us that all our hard work would pay off, and predicted that the queues for tickets would stretch right around the block. He added, 'No, that's not true. I meant to say *twice* around the block.' And, boy, was he right. Advanced bookings went through the roof and, if news of any returns at the box-office got out, it was like a bun fight, with people scrambling for tickets. It quickly became the hottest show in town.

Opening night

The Sound of Music opened at the Palace Theatre in London on 18 May 1961, and was headlined as a 'new' Rodgers and Hammerstein production. British audiences knew of its previous history on Broadway, of course, hence the demand for tickets.

On the first night Richard Rodgers stood at the side of the stage, wished everyone the best of luck, then grabbed Jean Bayliss' hand and said, 'Don't worry, I've not had a good review since *Oklahoma*.' And with that on she went!

Rodgers was always popping over from New York to see how we were all getting on; he made a point of keeping a metronome in the orchestra pit to ensure we never deviated from the set rhythm. He was a bit of a perfectionist in that respect.

With eight performances a week you pretty much lived the show, but while I always left my character at the theatre, one cast member in particular started to take her role a little too seriously.

Constance Shacklock gave a new meaning to the term 'method acting' by convincing herself she was a real-life Mother Abbess.

If you knocked on her dressing room door she would never say 'Come in' but would bellow 'Ave' in her deep contralto voice. After each performance her dressing room was transformed into a confessional. Cast members called in to have their sins absolved and my dresser, Elsie, often waited outside to see who would slip out, their cheeks glowing red with the embarrassment of what they'd just disclosed.

Constance had trained at the Royal Academy of Music and, as noted, had gone on to become a huge opera star. *The Sound of Music* was her first ever musical theatre role and we felt she looked down her nose at it (and us). She was always quick to remind people that she was 'a very well-respected opera singer' and performing in this musical was 'quite beneath her,' but she always tellingly added, 'The experience is good, as is the money.' Before we closed she actually admitted she had no regrets about taking the role. Her husband had died mid-run in August 1965 and I think the show was actually a godsend to her in keeping her mind otherwise occupied. I always got on very well with Constance and found her to be a very compassionate lady, but some of the other cast members were quite irritated by her condescending manner. Maybe because they had to go to confession many more times than me?

High spirits

I'm sure if you asked any actor they could recall tales of ghostly goings on while appearing in theatres up and down the country, from the spooky apparition in the stalls to the feeling you're being watched from the wings. Well, Olive Gilbert went one better.

You see, Olive was a great friend of Ivor Novello, the Welsh-born composer, singer and actor who became one of the most popular British entertainers of the first half of the 20th century. She even lived in the flat below him at the Strand Theatre in the Aldwych. Olive would tell anyone who would listen about strange noises coming from the flat above – footsteps, furniture being moved and a piano lid being slammed down. She was convinced it was 'dear Ivor', as she referred to him. Now I know that doesn't sound particularly bizarre in itself but let me add that Novello died in 1951!

Olive was one of life's eccentrics and would constantly try to regale us with stories about 'dear Ivor' as though they were still neighbours. It got to the point where, whenever she mentioned his name, we'd humour her and change the subject.

One day, after a matinée, Olive said, 'My darling, you are to take tea with me this afternoon at my flat. Dear Ivor would simply love to meet you.' With my curiosity pricked, I thought 'Why not?'

While Olive prepared tea I heard footsteps in the flat above. She was seemingly quite used to them and casually asked, 'Did you hear that?'

'Hear what?' I asked, pretending I hadn't, and picked up another crumpet.

'It's dear Ivor. He paces the floor when the lyrics don't come to him,' she replied.

It all sounded rather bizarre but strangely convincing. I wouldn't say I believed her but I didn't doubt her totally either. She'd once told me that when Novello died his flat had been left untouched, almost like a shrine, and was never sold or rented, so no one could possibly be up there. Could they? The footsteps continued and were followed by what sounded like furniture being dragged across the floor.

'That's dear Ivor saying hello,' said Olive. 'He's dragging the piano stool across the floor.'

The noise stopped just as suddenly as it had started, and was followed by an almighty crash. 'Oh, that's dear Ivor slamming the piano lid,' Olive explained. 'He gets into such a rage when the music just won't flow.'

By this time I was feeling a little uneasy. As Olive had a spare key to the flat above I suggested we took a peek. We crept upstairs and opened the flat's door. I was a little anxious, as I wasn't sure what to expect. Would there be a ghostly form of Ivor Novello pacing the floor? Or just an empty room? Sadly, it was the latter. However, the piano stool was in the centre of the floor, which seemed a little at odds with the rest of the room. I glanced at Olive and she gave me a knowing look. We never spoke a word, just closed the door and went back downstairs to finish our tea before heading back to the theatre.

Was she mad? Was *I* mad? Was it some elaborate hoax? I'll never know, but whenever Olive mentioned 'dear Ivor' again, I didn't dismiss her outlandish stories quite so readily!

Shaking the habit

Although I'd thoroughly enjoyed the sell-out year of *The Sound of Music*, I felt I didn't want to stay on any longer when I heard the show was being extended due to its huge popularity. I thought it time for a new challenge and declined to extend my contract. When the producers heard they were absolutely gobsmacked and questioned why I would consider leaving something that was so successful at the height of its popularity.

Olive Gilbert heard, too, and of course 'dear Ivor' had something to say about it. She said he told her, 'Never leave a successful show. You think the phone will start ringing but it won't and you'll regret it in the end.'

Of course the added bonus for me, being in London with fairly regular hours, was that I could spend lots of time with my mother and Pat, which wasn't always possible when I was touring or away filming. The show was such a golden goose that the producers offered me an increase in salary, an increase which I simply couldn't refuse! I am by no means a greedy person but any actor will tell you that this business is such an insecure one that you can't afford to turn down good offers of work. That, coupled with dear Ivor's advice, persuaded me to stay. God, who would believe

I based my career decisions on the advice of a man who died ten years earlier?

Anyhow, this round of 'don't leave us' negotiations continued year on year until I was told I was the highest paid actress in London's West End!

One cast member who ignored Olive's advice (and that of 'dear Ivor') was Silvia Beamish, who played the role of Sister Berthe while also understudying the Mother Abbess for Constance Shacklock. Silvia believed she was too big a talent just to play a lowly nun and would happily tell this to anyone who would listen. It reached the point where I told her that yes, she had a wonderful voice, and that one day she might make it big, but 'Until then just stop complaining and get on with the job you're signed up to do.'

Constance was a true professional and never missed a show, which only added to Silvia's frustration. Therefore, three months before the end of her contract, she announced, rather grandly and publicly, that she would be leaving the show.

Like the rest of us, she had initially signed to stay with the show for one year, no more, no less. When the producers reminded her of this fact she realised more drastic measures were needed. Knowing they would never tolerate the show getting any kind of bad publicity, she came up with the idea of being so outrageous she'd be fired on the spot.

Silvia was a big lady, not unlike Constance Shacklock, and one day after the matinée she left the theatre not only in full make-up but also wearing her fulsome nun's habit – something which was absolutely forbidden by the management. The next thing we knew, our stage manager, Gerry Phillips, received a phone call from a rather disgruntled local pub landlord.

'We've got one of your nuns here causing a bit of mayhem,' he said. 'She's drinking whisky and smoking cigars and behaving quite badly. Would you please come and remove her from my premises? It's bad for business.'

Gerry told the landlord he was on his break and would attend to the situation as soon as possible. Unimpressed, the landlord yelled 'I want her out of my pub now!' and slammed the phone down.

Gerry, whose duty it was to ensure no actresses left in costume, was in a bit of a panic; if word got out he'd be for the chop. Like all theatrical producers, the Rodgers and Hammerstein organisation were very protective of their shows' reputations and the family values they portrayed. Gerry saw the headline 'Nun in drunken rampage' flash before his eyes, so he dropped everything and hurried up Shaftesbury Avenue. By the time he arrived at the hostelry in question, out of breath, Silvia had left for the next pub. Apparently before she disappeared, a crowd had formed outside due to all the commotion and she was telling all and sundry that she was a real nun and to prove it belted out 'Climb Every Mountain' with a glass and cigar in hand. This had upset quite a few passers-by who were aghast at what they were witnessing. But on the other hand many people found her hugely entertaining and followed her down Shaftsbury Avenue, Pied Piper-like.

Gerry, head in hands, was absolutely livid. A stage-hand ran down to find him and said they'd been receiving more and more calls from angry pub landlords complaining that a rather rotund drunken nun was causing havoc and would they come and remove her. Gerry rushed onto the next pub but of course by the time he got there she'd made a run for it. The landlord had no idea in which direction she'd gone and didn't particularly care; he was more concerned about the customers leaving his hostelry in droves.

Eventually Gerry found her, absolutely paralytic, but still smoking a big cigar and singing 'Climb Every Mountain' at the top of her voice, much to the amazement of the customers. Perhaps in this case a better song choice might have been, 'How are we going to solve a problem like Silvia?'

The Hills Are Alive...

Gerry, along with an accompaniment of theatre staff, dragged Silvia back down Shaftsbury Avenue and through the stage door. The commissionaire took one look at the inebriated figure before him and said, 'Boy are you in trouble now.' And she slurred 'GOOD!'

Of course by this time word had spread and the management were waiting to give her a real dressing down. 'I'm an absolute disgrace,' she slurred while still puffing on her large cigar, 'and deserve to be fired. And, you know what, I don't give a damn.'

Her wish was granted and she was dismissed from the show immediately. From the moment she stumbled out, we thought we'd never see her again.

Slow dissolve...

A year or so later, I was in my dressing and there was a loud knock at the door. I asked 'Who is it?' and a voice replied, 'Eunice, it's Silvia, Silvia Beamish.'

The door flew open and in she walked. She'd lost stones in weight; her nails and hair were immaculate and she was dripping in mink and jewels. I was in total shock. The last time I'd seen her ahe was falling out of the stage door of the Palace Theatre.

'I thought I'd drop in and see how it was all going,' she said.

It turned out that her Equity card had been revoked and in those days you couldn't work in England unless you had one, so she decided to use her training as a Lieder singer and headed to Germany to look for work. She ended up singing in the chorus of an illustrious Lieder orchestra and, when one person took ill hours before a recording, she'd stepped forward and offered her services – and was reportedly magnificent. The conductor of the orchestra fell madly in love with her and with his guidance she became one of Germany's top Lieder singers.

Just think, if she hadn't gone on that drunken walkabout she'd have still been understudying. What a success story – good old

Silvia, I say. And Equity obviously forgave her sins as she returned to the West End in the early 1970s, playing Baroness Lehzen in *I and Albert*.

Cast notes

In 1963 Jean Bayliss decided to leave the show when her contract came to an end and was replaced by the lovely Sonia Rees, who had in fact also been in the company since we began.

Oh, and I should also mention Helen Wigglesworth, who was one of the original Von Trapp children. Aged 12, she auditioned for the part, got it, and stayed in London for the first nine months of the show. She is rather better known these days as Helen Worth of *Coronation Street* fame.

It was quite sad in that none of the children were allowed to speak to the main actors. That wasn't our idea but the management's. If they ever had to address us then it was always with 'Mr, Mrs or Miss' to preserve an air of respect, and they always had to curtsey too. That's all well and good, but, by putting such distance between us, the children never felt able to ask us questions or learn anything from our experience. And when you're working in the theatre or in film, there needs to be informality as you're all part of the same team, for goodness' sake. Anyhow, I learnt a lesson there and have ever since made a point of encouraging and speaking with younger co-stars.

In June of that year, something happened to cement my firm belief in fate and luck playing a huge part in life. Every matinée day for two years, I religiously left for home at 5.20 pm but on this one particular day I decided to take advantage of the beautiful weather and sun bathe on the roof of the Palace Theatre instead. Just as I reached the roof, I heard an almighty crash and commotion below. I looked over the side and saw a car had smashed into mine. (This was in the days when you could park in central London.) The police later explained that the driver's side of my vehicle was completely crushed, and if I had got into my car as usual that afternoon I'm sure I wouldn't be here today to tell this tale.

Makes you think, doesn't it?

Blind rage

A couple of months later, in August 1963, my career was thrown into jeopardy by a Venetian blind. (Please stop giggling at the back.)

I'd returned home after a matinée and, as it was a hot sticky summer's day, decided to have a shower. I pulled the cord to close the large blind in my bathroom and the whole thing came crashing down, hitting me directly in the face. There was blood everywhere and my screams alerted the porter downstairs, who came rushing up to see what was wrong. When he saw me, he took a step back, as though in horror, and then began reassuring me that everything would be OK.

His car was parked downstairs and he rushed me to hospital – not an ordinary hospital but the London Eye Hospital. I was immediately taken down for an operation which ended up involving 49 stitches; unbeknown to me, the blind had caught my eye and almost gouged it out of its socket. The surgeons did a fabulous job but later told me it was 'touch and go' as to whether I would lose my sight in that eye. A horrible thought.

A day or so later, while resting in hospital, I felt something moving under the covers and a small hand touching mine. A voice whispered, 'Don't worry, I've just had an operation and it was very good and now I can see again and I wanted to tell you not to worry and that everything will be all right.'

It was a little girl who'd sneaked in from the children's ward next door. She told me that her parents had taken her to see *The Sound of Music* for her birthday and how lovely it was, and how much they all enjoyed it. Of course I was bandaged up and couldn't see a thing so just had to imagine this cute little girl next to me. She knew she shouldn't really be there and scurried off back to the ward whenever the nurses approached. She became a regular visitor and a real tonic for me in those ten days before I was well enough to go home.

I did try and find her before I left, as I wanted to say goodbye and invite her and her parents to a backstage tour to meet all the cast. But sadly she'd been discharged just before me.

When I returned home there was a letter from the Venetian blind company saying how shocked they were after hearing about my accident, and offering to fit a brand-new blind free of charge. My faith in human nature had been restored not once, but twice.

I should mention that, totally coincidentally, a few days before the accident my understudy took me to one side and mentioned that her boyfriend was visiting at the weekend, and asked if I would mind 'pulling a sickie' so he could see her perform as Elsa in the show – because, you see, she'd already told him she was playing my part! I said it was 'out of the question'. I could never be that unprofessional.

Upon returning to the show, the cast and crew welcomed me back and all said they were so pleased my injuries weren't as serious as they might have been and how lucky I was and so on, when my understudy came bounding over.

'Thank you, Miss Gayson, thank you.'

'Sorry?'

'For throwing that sickie. Graham was *so* impressed with my performance!'

Unwelcome attention

The showbiz world seems to attract its fair share of oddballs and *The Sound of Music* was no exception. One night in my dressing room a thin envelope was pushed underneath my door. I picked it up, saw that it was empty and rushed outside. But there was nobody in sight.

Outside the dressing room there were very heavy soundproof doors, as it was near the stage, and they were moving slightly. I showed my dresser Elsie the envelope and she went very quiet.

'You might not have seen the ghost here but I have,' she said, as she'd been a dresser at the theatre for years, 'and I do know that one of her things is to put thin envelopes underneath the doors. And nobody has ever caught her doing it.'

Laughing it off, I thought it was a bit cheeky that a ghost should be offering me notes on my performance!

Then more and more envelopes appeared under my door, and these *did* contain letters – threatening letters. At first I thought somebody was playing a game, as they'd obviously heard about the first one, but these letters detailed how their author was going to do very, very nasty things to me. Although management alerted the police they never caught the person behind it as he/she seemed to know whenever the coast was clear – namely, when I was on stage and when Elsie wasn't in the dressing room but waiting in the wings for my quick change. We knew it had to be somebody front of house or backstage who had knowledge of the routine and running order of the show.

One night, when I was on stage and in the middle of a song, a blinding light suddenly hit my eyes. It was so intense that my top note shredded into three. The conductor looked at me as if I was going absolutely bananas, but every time I looked forward I was totally dazzled. Luckily it had happened very near the mid-way point, and as the curtain closed the stage manager came running on and asked, 'What the hell is going on?'

I said, 'The light, the light that was shining in my eyes. It almost blinded me.'

'What light?' he asked, looking around. 'There *is* no light on your eyes, you're imagining it.'

No one else knew what I was talking about, as no one else had been affected, so he all but dismissed me out of hand. 'Hang on, if it happens again I'm going to walk off stage,' I told him in an attempt to make him realise the seriousness of the matter. 'Someone was definitely throwing light into my eyes.'

The second half got underway and, sure enough, during my next big number the light came again and my notes began to split. The conductor started waving at me like mad. How I got through that song I'll never know. I later said to the stage manager, 'You know I'm not an hysteric but I swear to you that I was being blinded, and that caused my notes to split.'

'I've never heard of such a thing. We'd best get the theatre doctor to see if we can find out what's wrong with you.'

The only person who believed me was my dresser Elsie. 'This is not like you, Miss Gayson,' she said. 'There's something happening here and it's not nice... it's very evil.' By this time, I was totally confused and began to doubt myself, but then wondered if it was the theatre's ghost. Well, what other reasoning was there?

I got myself dressed to come down for the finale but when I reached the stage doorkeeper's kiosk Elsie was already there, talking about what had happened. She suddenly screamed, 'Miss Gayson, fall to the floor. He's got a knife' and without thinking I just dropped to the floor. Elsie and Gerry grabbed the man, who had indeed got a knife in his hand.

He was a member of the orchestra who had mentally flipped. In fact, he told the police and ambulance crews that I had been talking about him on stage. I'd never even met a single member of the orchestra but he'd got this thing in his head that, when I delivered lines on stage, they were directed at him personally. They made further enquiries and discovered that he'd been the one slipping notes under my door and had done exactly the same thing to an actress at the Palladium three years earlier. He had a mirror and directed the arc lamps directly into her eyes, from below, while she was singing – just as he had me.

The last I heard he was carted off to a psychiatric hospital, never to be seen again.

In another oddball event, one afternoon three policemen turned up at my dressing room and told me to 'Sit down' as they had some very bad news for me. Of course, I panicked, thinking my mother or sister had been involved in an accident. But what they went on to tell me was beyond belief. They said they were 'sorry' to inform me my father had died.

I told them he'd died many years ago and it couldn't possibly be him, and any member of my family would corroborate this. It turned out this man, who lived in St Albans, told all his friends that I was his daughter and, apparently, I'd got too 'big' to acknowledge him any longer. I'd supposedly told him he was dead in my eyes, so he plastered his walls with my photographs to 'remember his daughter'.

I never dared visit St Albans for years afterwards as I was afraid that everyone would hate me for being so horrid to my father!

Odds-on winner

By May 1964 we had reached our 1264th performance and had broken the record for the longest running production at the Palace Theatre, beating *King's Rhapsody*. One and three quarters of a million people had already seen us and advance bookings were being taken up until Christmas. A year later, bookings were still healthy and the show's popularity seemed never ending. I'd meet friends in the street and they'd ask 'Are you working?' and I'd say 'Yes, I'm in *The Sound of Music* at the Palace' and they'd say 'Oh, is that *still* running?' 'Oh yes,' I'd say.

1965 was a year in which I managed to cause controversy not once, but twice. In January I was approached to become a racing tipster for ITV's new flagship Saturday afternoon *World of Sport* programme, which was in direct competition with the BBC's *Grandstand*. It all came about after my dresser Elsie, who used to like a bet on the horses every Saturday, said there was a big race coming up one afternoon and would I like to put a few bob on? I said I wouldn't even know how to, as I wasn't a gambler. She said, 'I'll read you some names of the runners and tell me what you fancy...'

My call came to go on stage and as I was walking down I saw a red London bus drive past the window. Elsie followed me, reading the names, and one of the horses was 'Red' something or other. 'That's it,' I said. 'I'll have that one!'

'How much, Miss Gayson?' Elsie asked. 'I think I'll have a couple of bob myself.'

'Oh, I don't know, make it 50 then,' I said as I dashed on stage.

Elsie laid the bet through the stage doorman (who called his bookmaker friend) – not for 50 bob but 50 pounds! Imagine my surprise when I was told my outsider had romped home at 40-1.

'Miss Gayson, Miss Gayson. You've won two thousand quid!' Elsie exclaimed during the interval.

The news spread like wildfire, and I felt obliged to organise a party for the cast and crew, which in turn hit the gossip columns. Next thing I knew, my agent called asking me if I wanted to try out for a pundit's job on this new TV sports programme! I told the producers my experience of horses was limited to a nasty encounter with one while shooting *The Revenge of Frankenstein*, but they seemed more interested in a famous face attracting female viewers than whether I could predict the winner of the 2.30 at Newmarket.

I thought it sounded like fun but, before ITV would commit, I had to agree to a few test runs. I was given a list of runners at Sandown one particular weekend and was asked to predict the 1st, 2nd and 3rd races. I had no particular method for choosing the horses other than my own instinct and whether I liked the sound of their names. No one could believe it when my first and second choices romped home. A second trial proved just as astonishing and ITV offered me a contract on the spot.

Initially they wanted me to appear at a racecourse every Saturday but of course my theatre commitments didn't allow much time for that, so in the end they devised a two-way link between me and the studio using a live broadcast unit outside the theatre. It worked quite well and my success rate was alarmingly good, so much so they then offered me a new (improved) deal, though one which stipulated I had to appear in person at a racecourse – flying in by helicopter and then getting back to the theatre in the nick of time for the performance. After a few weeks of this dashing to-and-fro the theatre management started worrying that if the weather turned I'd be stranded and wouldn't make it back in time for the show. So when ITV offered me a long-term contract the Rodgers and Hammerstein organisation refused permission. I am sure the BBC and Britain's bookmakers breathed a sigh of relief – I must have cost them thousands!

The presenter of BBC's *Grandstand* at the time, David Coleman, held a press conference where he stated that 'A glamour girl picking winners with a hat pin is an insult to women viewers.' I disagreed and even wrote a letter to the *Evening Standard* stating, 'I think a lot of people pick horses my way and in the two pilot shows I managed to pick four winners out of six races.' Not bad!

But the row went on, and David Coleman persisted in stirring the press by saying, 'Women are interested in serious sport. Women are quite happy to watch me – I don't find them running away from me, on or off the screen. We have been doing our programme for six years – you can't beat that sort of experience. We have seen off all sorts of challenges from ITV. In the end, it's not the commentator that matters, it's the sports events. We have the best events and ITV can't hide that, in spite of the bright packaging.'

No sour grapes there!

An honest mistake

On 14 April 1965 something happened which led to great personal embarrassment. I was driving through Hove in my Ford Capri and was pulled over by a local policeman, who explained that he was doing random checks to make sure road fund licences weren't out of date. It must have been his lucky day as my licence had expired on 31 March and was indeed two weeks out of date. I explained that I'd simply forgotten to renew it.

On 1 May, as instructed by Brighton and Hove police, I sent a cheque to the Greater London Council licensing authority to cover the period of April to July and thought that would be the last of it. How wrong I was.

The police decided to proceed with a prosecution and a summons was served to me personally. It stated if I didn't want to appear in court on 7 October I could simply mark the form 'pleading guilty' and send it off. I figured this would be the best course of damage limitation – as I knew too well, the Rodgers and Hammerstein organisation would not be pleased about the bad publicity a star of their show would receive if I appeared in court. Little did I know that my plea in writing was never received, thanks to the Post Office losing it, and as I failed to appear on 7 October a warrant was issued for my arrest.

Of course, it wasn't difficult for the police to find me – my name was in four-foot flashing letters on the front of the Palace Theatre. On 3 November they kindly let me finish the matinée performance and then arrested me. They took me to Tottenham Court Road police station and, after being cautioned, I was bailed for the princely sum of £5 pending an appearance at Hove Magistrates' Court. Of course, word got out and journalists from all over the world were ringing my agent – though, not understanding the British legal system, most of them thought I must have committed some dastardly crime. When they heard the real reason they thought it was a farce that I'd been charged for such a trivial misdemeanour. Join the club, I thought.

The very next evening I attended a charity function at the Dorchester Hotel and was amused to hear people whispering 'She's out, she's out,' as if I were some master criminal who had evaded the judiciary. The case was described by my barrister as 'trivial and petty' and this was reflected in the outcome, as I went to court and was fined just £1. Can you believe the indignity of it all!

Backstage visitors

When someone said Jimmy Logan was in Roger Dann's dressing room after the show one evening I thought, 'He's bound to come and see me,' as really I had launched my career at his family theatre.

Though, for some reason, he didn't. I was really upset afterwards. I'd always acknowledged the fact that, if I hadn't played at his theatre's amateur night, I wouldn't have gone on to a career as an actor. Maybe he thought I wouldn't remember him now I was a West End star? Whatever, it was a real shame. Our paths never crossed again, and I never had the chance to thank him.

Laurence Olivier, however, used to come once a week with his children, though if he was working it'd be once a month, and he usually popped backstage for a chat to tell us all how much he still loved it. Larry wasn't the only one, as by 1966 some two and a half million people had paid £2 million to see *The Sound of Music*; we'd run longer than any other Rodgers and Hammerstein musical!

Unfortunately, as with all good things, the run did eventually come to end. We closed on 14 January 1967, five years, nine months and 2385 performances later. I was there for the first and the last show.

We became the second longest running musical (beaten only by *Oliver!*), which wasn't bad for something that had initially been panned by the critics. The whole cast had spent so much time together both on and off stage that we were like a family. We witnessed births, deaths, marriages and breakdowns; you name it, we saw it. I have to say it was one of the most fun and rewarding times of my life; it was never a chore as the music and lyrics were so enchanting. Of course, it was hard work, performing eight shows a week (not including extra charity performances). But we never complained and just got on with it. Rodgers and Hammerstein were never happy about time off and wouldn't allow holidays if they weren't legally obliged; this was only resolved very late in the run when Equity negotiated a statutory holiday allowance. Boy, was I glad of that. Looking back, I must have only taken five weeks holiday during the whole run!

A week after we closed I checked into a health hydro for a well-earned rest. I didn't realise just how exhausted I was, but thankfully the show had afforded me the luxury of financial solvency.

Chapter Eight

I Admire Your Luck, Mr... ?
My adventures with 007

L ittle did I know that a few days filming back in 1962 would change my life; in fact, that one film sparked a phenomenon that's still going strong 50 years on. When I think of all the TV and theatre work I've done over the years, yet I'm still best remembered for my association with the James Bond films – the easiest and most joyous film work I've ever done. It's extraordinary, and not a bad legacy to be remembered by!

The $1 million budget for *Dr No* is a mere fraction of the cost of today's films, yet – modest though it may have been, given the scope of the production – at the time it was an incredible amount of money. While a close eye was kept on the purse strings, the producers and director had a relatively free rein, so things were very different compared to nowadays: days were a little more easy-going, slightly but happily chaotic and always punctuated with lots of laughter and fun. Back then nobody had coined the phrase 'health and safety'. Mind you, the unions were a bit of a pain. They wouldn't much mind an effects chap climbing into the rafters with a stick of dynamite in his back pocket, but if a prop man switched on a hose pipe, rather than calling in a plumber to do it, then everyone was called out on strike.

If anyone involved in the first Bond film said that 007 would become a worldwide sensation, let alone spawn a franchise of 23 films, countless spin-offs in computer games, books, merchandising and DVDs etc, then they were certainly fantasising!

Slow dissolve...

It was 3 November 1961, and I remember to this day Sean Connery being announced as the actor chosen to play James Bond in a series – they hoped! – of films based on the Ian Fleming books. Sean wasn't the first choice of producers Cubby Broccoli and Harry Saltzman, far from it. Other names that had been mentioned included Patrick McGoohan, Richard Johnson, James Mason, Rex Harrison, David Niven, Trevor Howard and even Cary Grant.

Cubby and Harry were very well-established and respected film producers in the UK, despite neither of them being British. Cubby was an American of Italian descent, and Harry a Canadian. Separately they had produced great films such as *Hell Below Zero*, *The Trials of Oscar Wilde*, *Saturday Night and Sunday Morning*, *Cockleshell Heroes*, *Look Back in Anger* and *The Entertainer*.

Harry secured a six-month option on the Fleming books in 1961, though Cubby had also been drawn to 007's adventures and, upon learning Harry had a fast-running-out option, suggested they form a partnership. Eon Productions was born, and the producers approached Columbia Pictures with their plans. They were turned down flat. Cubby then called his old friend Arthur Krim at United Artists who suggested the duo fly to New York to meet him. Alas, Harry didn't have the airfare and had to ask his new partner to loan it him; despite both of them having had moderate financial success in movies, neither was by any means rich. Everything was riding on them making a deal, and make a deal they did – for a series of five pictures.

With a script, a director – Terence Young, who had collaborated with Cubby previously – and money in their pockets, the producers were just lacking one thing: their James Bond. On the suggestion of Peter Hunt, they looked at a film called *On the Fiddle*, which Peter had edited, and saw Sean Connery. Coincidentally

Left: Bond Girl number one, Sylvia Trench! Modelling the famous red dress, which was actually a last-minute replacement held together with clothes pegs.

Below: Unlucky at cards ... but lucky in love. Making a date with Sean Connery's 007 in *Dr No*.

A hole in one! It was so liberating to play a sexy character in *Dr No* rather than the bland, twee, chaste types seen in other British films of the early 1960s.

Above: Soon after *Dr No* I had my first role in ITC's *The Saint.* Here I am in *The Invisible Millionaire.*

Right: Messing about on the river. Back with Sean in *From Russia With Love.*

Opposite: Terence Young gives Sean and I a few suggestions for playing our scene, which featured (below) one of the first bleepers and mobile phones ever seen.

Right: On location ... at Elstree Studios. Posing for another ITC show, *Danger Man*, in 1964.

Below: Quick, quick, slow ... Dance lessons with Patrick Macnee in *The Avengers*.

Above: With Roger Moore and George Murcell in my second encounter with *The Saint* – this one was called *The Saint Bids Diamonds*.

Right: A promotional photo for Stephen Sondheim's *Into the Woods*.

Top: My daughter Kate followed in my footsteps with Pierce Brosnan's 007 in 1995's *GoldenEye*.

Left: Kate with her son Morgan, my first grandchild.

Above: And here is Morgan, all grown up, with his sister Jessica – my lovely granddaughter.

At the London Palladium in 2008, celebrating 100 years of Ian Fleming. Left to right: Zena Marshall, Tania Mallett, Caroline Munro, Sir Roger Moore, Shirley Eaton, me and the delightful Madeline Smith.

Opening the Bond in Motion exhibition at Beaulieu in 2012. Left to right: Ralph Montagu, me, Britt Ekland, Jenny Hanley and Madeline Smith.

Cubby's wife Dana had seen a Disney film called *Darby O'Gill and the Little People*, and came home raving about this young Scottish actor. With their start date looming they decided to call Sean in for a meeting; however, he refused to audition for them, believing his body of work was sufficient.

Terence had always maintained they needed someone 'ballsy' in the part. Sean was a big, tough-looking man who was slightly arrogant and had a devil-may-care attitude. But, above all else, he moved gracefully like a cat. He was absolutely perfect.

The producers were sure they had their 007. However, their backers at UA didn't agree, as you can see in a telegram from Eon's archive:

```
8/23/61
  L/T
  Harry Saltzman — Warwickfilm — London
  Blumofe reports New York did not care
  for Connery feels we can do better
                              CUBBY
```

Cubby, Harry and Terence Young shot a screen test with Sean (which has since become the Holy Grail that no one can find), and remained adamant that he was the only actor to play Bond.

Toga! Toga! Toga!

I first became aware of Sean Connery after seeing him in a small picture called *Hell Drivers*, which was made at Pinewood around the time I was under contract to Rank and co-starred my friend Peggy Cummins. I thought he had an incredible on-screen presence, but it was such a small role hardly anyone took any notice.

Then, one day in 1959, I was in Oxford for a meeting and noticed Sean was performing in *The Bacchae* at the Oxford Playhouse. Remembering his performance in *Hell Drivers* I decided to stay on and check it out; it was a Greek tragedy and he was playing the part of Pentheus. Well, let me tell you, he had the most incredible body and looked absolutely fantastic dressed in a toga. It wasn't only a case of brawn but brains too, as his performance was an absolute knockout. I thought then we'd be seeing and hearing a lot more of him in the future, albeit not as much as I'd seen of him in a toga.

A couple of years later, Sean became a friend of my former husband, Leigh Vance, who'd recently cast him in his film *The Frightened City*. Leigh, with whom I was still on friendly terms, had arranged for us all to meet for dinner. Sean couldn't honestly believe he'd got the Bond role. He thought the producers were out of their minds casting him in such a suave and debonair part; he was nothing like James Bond, just a normal casual guy who wore jeans and a donkey jacket. I told him not to worry as I knew someone involved with the film, who would steer him in the right direction and, in fact, make him an international star.

You see, shortly before, on a typical rainy day in London, I was at home wondering if I should bother trying to brave the elements when the phone rang. It was Terence Young, with whom I'd previously worked on *Zarak*, and he explained he'd been lined up to direct the first James Bond film, going on to say that if this film was a success they planned to produce a further five and that he would direct them all. He added that, as I was his 'good luck charm', I had to be involved. I was a little taken aback. 'Well, when I am with you or do a film with you there are never any problems and other people seem to bring me bad luck,' he explained. 'You'll bring a bit of class to the proceedings too,' he added.

I was so flattered Terence thought of me in such a way. I was, and am, very modest and find it quite hard to take any kind of compliment. However, the idea of working with him again and being involved with something so intriguing and exciting was a thrilling prospect. While my lips were saying 'Yes, yes, yes,' there was a niggling in the back of my mind. I was tied to a year-long contract playing Elsa Schraeder in the London production of *The Sound of Music* and I knew Rodgers and Hammerstein would never let me get involved in anything which would take me out of the show for any length of time. They didn't mind one-off TV shows, but longer extracurricular work was a real no-no. I didn't say anything to Terence at first, other than 'Yes, yes, yes,' and broached the subject of being released for a film with the theatre management.

They immediately suggested I was trying to get out of my contract, which was ridiculous as I didn't even know the schedule of the Bond film at that point, and whether it was one day or five. Though I have to admit that anything that takes you out of a long-running show for a day or two is a great relief from the monotony of it. I then confided in Terence that I thought I had a 'problem with management'. He was always very inventive and, thinking on his feet, told me not to worry as the part involved just a couple of days filming at Pinewood, after which, he assured me, I'd be whisked back to London in time for the theatre show each evening.

He went on to say he had me in mind for one of two characters, with his old friend Lois Maxwell playing the other. However, Lois was rather conservative in her values and upon realising the requirement of some semi-nudity with one of the two characters on offer, she made it clear she was only interested in the other – Moneypenny.

'You'll be playing a girl called Sylvia Trench, James Bond's love interest,' Terence told me. Apparently they wanted to 'sex the film up a little' in the first reel, so had written this part with a view to it becoming a recurring one. These days an actress appearing wearing a shirt and a pair of knickers wouldn't cause anyone to flinch, but 50 years ago it was considered rather daring and Lois Maxwell just didn't care for it. Though it was later suggested that my 'fulsome proportions' as well as my acting ability would have seen me play Sylvia over Moneypenny in any event.

I asked who I'd be acting with. 'Oh, a young actor called Sean Connery,' Terence replied. Thoughts of Sean in *that* toga clouded my mind!

Terence went on to explain that Sylvia would appear briefly in each new Bond adventure and just as they were about to 'get down to it' he'd be bleeped away on another mission to save the world from the clutches of some criminal mastermind. By the time of the second film I'd be out of *The Sound of Music* and appearing as a regular wouldn't be an issue. I even imagined that one day I could become Mrs James Bond. Sadly, things didn't really turn out that way, but more on that later.

Terence was himself an ex-agent so he knew the spy game. He always arrived on set dressed immaculately and I used to joke that he was on the wrong side of the camera and could have easily played the role himself. He certainly knew what made a special agent and how they would react to certain situations; experience which was invaluable to the young Sean Connery.

Prior to shooting, Terence took Sean under his wing and introduced him to the finest tailors where all his clothes were handmade, including his shirts and shoes. He ate the finest foods and drank the finest wines at the best restaurants in town. He wanted Sean to be familiar with the life of the suave worldly-wise spy he was about to portray, and comfortable in his new outfits. Exchanging his jeans and a donkey jacket for tailor-made suits was a bit of a culture shock, so Terence suggested Sean sleep in his new clothes until he felt totally at ease and comfortable in them.

I hadn't been to Pinewood for a few years, not really since I was released from my dreaded Rank contract, and was amazed at the difference in the studio. Gone was the closed-shop Rank production line, and in came a fresh bunch of people hiring space, including Disney, Peter Rogers and his Carry On films, and of course Eon Productions. It was actually through *Dr No's* production designer, Ken Adam, that Pinewood was chosen. Although Ken preferred working at Shepperton, he knew that a smaller studio simply couldn't cope with his needs on this film, whereas Pinewood was much better geared for an epic production.

Off the peg

My first day's shoot did not go smoothly, and my reputation for being Terence's good luck charm was left hanging in the balance. The interior set, based loosely on London's famous Les Ambassadeurs club, had been built on Pinewood Studios' D stage by Ken Adam, and dressed lavishly with brown and beige decor and adornments. I walked onto the set in my beautiful brown and gold silk dress, which had been specially made for the film, and Terence hit the roof.

Though we'd had a run through, and I'd popped on set for lighting requirements, this was the first time I'd been seen in costume... and I blended in totally with the background!

'No, no, no,' Terence shouted, with his hands sliding up over his head. 'This scene is absolutely pivotal to the whole film, as we're introduced to James Bond for the very first time, and I can't see her!' He went on to castigate some young girl from the costume department, saying, 'It's important she wears something striking that stands out.'

I was swiftly and silently dispatched to the studio wardrobe department, but they simply didn't have anything suitable off the peg. Creating another dress from scratch would have held up shooting, and cost a fortune, so that was out. It was a disaster and I dreaded to think how much the mistake was now costing in terms of wasted time.

With panic setting in, I, along with the wardrobe mistress, was sent down to the local village to try and find something – anything. I knew from my Rank days that there was a little dress shop down there but as we pulled up outside my heart sank; it had become a wool shop. Nevertheless we were there and felt duty-bound to ask if the owner had anything. The little old lady behind the counter said she didn't and couldn't really help, but as we were about to leave I noticed a beautiful bright red georgette dress hanging on the back of the door. It was one of those eureka moments you hear about. I asked the shopkeeper who it was for and she told us she'd had it made as a favour for a lady who never came back. She pulled it down and I saw it was a size 20. At the time I was a size eight, but we were so desperate I tried the dress on; of course, it absolutely drowned me, but the colour was so perfect.

With time still ticking we decided we'd take it back to the studio, and there the wardrobe mistress made some hasty adjustments. I joined everyone back on the set in what you now know as the beautiful, striking red dress. Terence expressed his wholehearted approval and we were off again.

'Right, and... Action!'

My first scene with Sean was inside the casino at the baccarat table and to say he was nervous would be an understatement. All I had to do was look up to see this gorgeous guy and deliver the line 'I admire your luck, Mr... ?' To which Sean should have replied 'Bond, James Bond.' Simple, or so you might think...

Nine takes later Sean had gone through every permutation of 'Bond, James Bond' you could think of, from 'Bond, Sean Bond' to 'Sean, Bond James' to 'James, I mean Bond James' and so on.

Now you have to remember that this was the big scene which introduced Sean Connery to world audiences and he had to convince them he was a cool, suave and intelligent super-spy. Cubby and Harry went from looking excited and hopeful, to appearing totally nonplussed and worried about whether they'd made the right choice. Of course their frustration only added to and compounded Sean's nerves.

I Admire Your Luck, Mr...?

Terence was silently pulling his hair out in frustration. It was now approaching lunchtime and it seemed like a good idea to break. Terence took me to one side and said, 'Eunice, please take Sean down to the restaurant and give him a couple of drinks. Calm him down and then we'll go again.' In those days Sean didn't really drink and one of my golden rules has always been never to drink when I'm working, as for one thing it just makes me feel sleepy, let alone anything else.

I grabbed Sean's arm and said, 'Come on, Sean, let's go for a drink. I need something to calm my nerves.'

He couldn't believe what he was hearing. 'You... drinking! I don't believe it! I need the drink, I'm the one who's nervous,' he said.

We went down to the Pinewood restaurant and ordered a couple of vodkas. I knew what would happen if I drank it all back, so I sipped mine slowly; Sean, meanwhile, grabbed his and gulped it down in one. 'How about we have another?'

'No thanks,' I replied. 'You're drinking far too fast for me.'

Regardless, Sean ordered two more and again downed his in one. When he wasn't looking I secretly tipped the contents of mine into a plant pot behind us. It was like one of those Ray Cooney comedy moments!

Just as he was about to order a third I realised he was drinking on an empty stomach and, being terrified of the consequences suggested we had some lunch. He said he wasn't hungry and would just have another drink. Mercifully, I managed to convince him to force a little food down, after which he got up and walked back to the stage as straight as a dye.

Sean was now pretty relaxed and was even cracking jokes with the crew. It seemed a drop (or three) of alcohol had done the trick and he was ready for anything. Terence called for silence, we re-set and the call of 'Action!' went up. I delivered the first part of the line, and Sean nailed it in one – 'The name's Bond. James Bond.'

Terence shouted 'Cut!' and was absolutely thrilled. He whispered to me, 'See, I told you. You're lucky for me.'

We went for the second take, as is the norm in films, to make sure the editor has a choice and also as a back-up in case anything happened to the film stock when processing. Mind you, Terence rarely shot more than he needed and in fact often shot a scene so tightly, without any extra coverage or spare takes, that he knew it would be edited exactly as he shot it.

OK, I deliver the first part of the line and Sean replies, 'Bond. James Bond. Miss… ?'

'Trench, Eunice Trench,' I replied. Now I was the one who blew it, after being word perfect all morning! Everyone on the set roared with laughter, which really broke the ice after a very stressful morning, and from then on Sean was word perfect – as was I. But I'll tell you something, I have never taken a drop of drink again during working hours.

The next day's scene involved me walking up to James Bond as he was preparing to leave the club to report to M's office. I had to present him with my card and 'be suggestive'. If you watch very closely you'll notice I'm walking quite stiffly across the set, the reason being that the hasty adjustments to the stunning red dress involved the addition of a few clothes pegs. Which was fine when I was sitting at the card table, but the cameraman, Ted Moore, pointed out that when standing I couldn't turn too far one way or the other or they would be in shot.

So there am I on the set of a $1 million film, in a beautiful red gown held together with pegs. But it was a beautiful tight fit and I thoroughly recommend it to anyone in need of urgent costume alterations!

A hole in one

Sylvia then sneaked into Bond's hotel room and cheekily dressed in one of his shirts, and little else, and that's where we next meet

her on film, pitching golf balls into a hat – time after time. I
thought it was ridiculous as not only had I never played golf in my
life but I didn't even know how to hold the club, so how on earth
was I supposed to sink each ball in one?

Sean and Terence were golf mad which made me even more
nervous. Terence reassured me that it would all work out, as they
had a golf expert standing by and that all I needed to do was aim
in the general direction of the hat; they'd then cut for the golf
expert to be inserted into the shot. Sean doubted he could get the
ball in the hat, never mind me – a great confidence booster!

On the first take, I hit the ball and it rolled straight into the
hat. Sean couldn't believe his eyes and doubled over laughing.
Terence was furious because he'd ruined the shot, but he too saw
the funny side and ended up screaming with laughter. We went
for a second take and Terence said, 'If by a fluke she does it again
and anybody laughs, they are fired and will have to leave the set
immediately.' I didn't really think too much about it, swung the
club back slightly and just hoped I'd hit the ball.

Surprise, surprise! I did it again and the ball shot straight into
the hat. The crew dared not laugh, but Sean fell about laughing
again, knowing full well that Terence couldn't possibly fire the
leading man.

With my filming complete, Terence kissed me goodbye and
thanked me for helping relax his leading man into the role. I
hopped into my car and headed back to London for the evening
show of *The Sound of Music*, not really thinking too much more
about the film.

Fast forward to 5 October 1962. *Dr No* had its world premiere
gala screening at the London Pavilion (now the Trocadero
centre) and I had to get permission to attend from Rodgers
and Hammerstein. Here I was again, this actress who was
more interested in a little spy film than performing in their
distinguished production, and they flatly refused as it would

have taken me out of the show for the night, and they'd have had to put my understudy on (who'd get paid a few extra quid as a result). Their attitude really annoyed me as I'd never missed a show, and this was the first time I'd asked for an evening off. I told them straight, 'I'm sorry but I'm going anyway.' I didn't hear another thing about it.

I'd been to many opening nights before but I really didn't know what to expect from this, as we'd had mixed reviews in the trade papers and even Ian Fleming himself described the film as 'Dreadful. Simply dreadful.' Though he later warmed to Sean and gave Bond a Scottish ancestry in his subsequent books.

I wore a fabulous pale pink satin dress which had been made for the last Venice Film Festival I'd attended, and was designed by a man at Berman's costumiers in London. Despite being a little late with my *Zarak* costumes, they had a client list as long as your arm, encompassing some of the biggest names of the entertainment world from Richard Burton to Roger Moore, Elizabeth Taylor and Sean Connery to name but a few. You knew with Berman's you would always get something very special indeed and they always made my gowns for film premieres and festivals; they were incredible but the only downside was I had to send them back afterwards.

I arrived at the Pavilion and could see that the police were having trouble holding the crowds back. As I was walked into the theatre, I noticed this dear little man fighting his way to the front shouting, 'Miss Gayson, Miss Gayson!' Of course, the police wouldn't let him through so I went over; it was chaos. He explained that he'd designed and made the dress I was wearing, and I eventually persuaded the police to let him through. In fact, the crowd opened like Moses parting the red sea so this dear little unassuming man could step through. His face lit up, while the people in the crowd were presumably wondering who the hell he was. I told him that he should be the one attending the premiere for making me such a beautiful dress and invited him in as my guest. I told him what a wonderful designer he was, to which he simply replied, 'Yeah, I'm not bad am I?'

We made it into the theatre through the bustling crowd and took our seats as the screen burst into life. The whole thing, from the first frame in Jamaica, looked incredible and Sean was simply fantastic, with his charisma bursting out of the screen. The audience had never seen anything quite like this – the glamorous locations, beautiful girls, crazed villain and amazing sets. You have to remember there was no such thing as low-cost travel back then and the ordinary man in the street had never been abroad; plus the staple fare on offer in British cinemas was dreary kitchen sink dramas or period pieces. Audiences were thirsty for something else, and *Dr No* delivered it by the bucket load – not least when Ursula Andress emerged in that swimming costume!

After the final credits rolled I realised a new star had been born. The film received rapturous applause and we were all gobsmacked, Sean most of all; he just couldn't believe the reaction.

The after party took place at the Savoy Hotel, where I met the lovely Zena Marshall properly for the first time. Although we appeared in the same film, we never shared a scene nor was I around the studio when she filmed her sequences. We had been together for half a day after the production wrapped to shoot some publicity photographs with Sean and Ursula Andress, but it was such a hectic day that we barely had a chance to talk. That night, though, we did. She told me that Sean had asked her to accompany him after he and his wife, Diane Cilento, had argued over something or other and she had flatly refused to attend the screening and party.

Zena and I became lifelong friends until her untimely death in 2009 from cancer. We travelled the world for autograph shows and conventions, and in August 2008 took part in the Ian Fleming Centenary celebrations at the London Palladium, where we both appeared on stage. Zena never mentioned her illness to me and it came as a huge shock to hear she had died a few months later. She was a true lady, brave, dignified with a wonderful sense of humour.

Her funeral, a full Catholic mass, was held at the Brompton Oratory and, while hugely sad, was one of the most uplifting services I have ever attended. I still miss Zena to this day.

007 returns

Three days after the gala screening of *Dr No*, the film was released across the United Kingdom and became a huge success. Rodgers and Hammerstein were happy as it ensured people came to see me in their show and the theatre was packed for months on end! The USA was a slightly different story though, as the film didn't make much of an initial impact, but enough to turn a nice profit. So plans were announced for a sequel, *From Russia With Love* (one of President John F Kennedy's listed top ten novels of all time, so deemed a natural choice by the producers). I would be reprising my role of Sylvia Trench, which rather bizarrely – given the great upturn in ticket sales following *Dr No* – annoyed Rodgers and Hammerstein. Maybe they were concerned I'd turn my back on the theatre if more film offers came in?

The pressure was on Eon, and United Artists doubled the budget to $2 million. Harry, Cubby and Terence knew that they had to up the game and build on the success of *Dr No* with even more glamorous locations, sets, outlandish villains and nail-biting stunts.

For my one scene, we filmed on the banks of the river Thames in the beautiful Berkshire village of Hurley. It was a lovely summer's day, and Bond and Sylvia were canoodling in a boat on one of his rare days off. But of course the inevitable happened and he was called away again to save the world, by means of a innovative bleeper device – a forerunner of pagers as we know them now. He phoned HQ from his car radio phone, but did tell them he'd be a little longer than first suggested, reporting in person after a little suggestive teasing from Sylvia!

I Admire Your Luck, Mr...?

The Royal Gala premiere of *From Russia With Love* was held on 10 October 1963 at the Odeon Leicester Square (which became the traditional home of future Bond premieres) in the presence of the Duke and Duchess of Bedford, with a separate simultaneous screening at the London Pavilion. Sean attended the premiere accompanied by leading lady Daniela Bianchi, producers Broccoli and Saltzman, and various celebrities of the day. This time round Rodgers and Hammerstein were insistent; they tolerated my day-time filming activities, but would not release me from my theatre contract to attend the premiere. While everyone else was sipping champagne and nibbling on canapés I was singing my heart out on the stage of the Palace Theatre.

It was April 1964 before the film opened in the USA, and boy did James Bond make an impact – so much so, *Dr No* was later re-released on a double-bill with it. In fact, *From Russia With Love* was a runaway success, exceeding *Dr No*'s $60 million worldwide take by almost $20 million. Quite naturally, a third film, *Goldfinger*, was moved into pre-production.

Terence saw the films as real money-spinners and felt their success was in no small part due to him, so he suggested to the producers that he receive a piece of the action – that is to say, a percentage of the profits. The producers flatly refused, saying there were only two partners in Eon Productions, so Terence pulled out.

Guy Hamilton was brought in to direct and quickly quashed any preconceived ideas about Bond, wanting to start afresh and put his own mark on the series. Unfortunately for me that meant no more Sylvia Trench, and any ambitions of her one day walking up the aisle to become Mrs James Bond were no more. But, hey, that's showbusiness.

Guess who?

To this day, fans still ask me if I ever kept in touch with Sean. I'd like to say I did but sadly it's not the case. The only time we ever really met again was when I owned a house in Spain, Majorca to be precise. My daughter Kate would have been about 14 or 15 years old at the time and like a lot of young girls swooned over Sean's son Jason, who had just taken over the title role in a very popular TV programme called *Robin of Sherwood*. Jason had long blonde hair and was every bit as handsome and gorgeous as his father.

One day Kate ran into the house hyperventilating. Eventually calming her down, I asked what was wrong. She said, 'I've... I've... I've just seen Jason Connery.'

'Of course you have darling, now don't be silly and settle down,' I replied.

'I have... I have. He's just driven into that house over the road in a white Rolls-Royce,' she said excitedly, and begged me to go and get his autograph.

I began to think it might possibly have been Jason after all, as I knew that the house had recently changed hands and no Spaniard in his right mind would be seen driving a Rolls-Royce, let alone a white one. We walked across the road and stood behind the hedge, listening, and we heard Sean's unmistakable voice. I shouted 'Hello' and the talking stopped.

I said, 'It's me, Eunice. Eunice Gayson.'

'Eunice Gayson? What the hell are you doing here?' Sean bellowed.

'I live over the road.'

The bushes parted and there was Sean.

'My God, we bought this house to get away from people and be incognito!'

I said, 'If you want to be incognito you'd better get rid of that white Rolls-Royce!'

Even in the early days Sean was a very private person and hated the attention stardom brought him. But, ever the gentleman, he invited us in and we spent the afternoon catching up. Kate not only got to meet Jason but spent the afternoon lazing around the swimming pool with him; she was so overcome she nearly drowned several times.

Oh! Actually there was one more instance when our paths crossed. A few years ago I was involved in a big Cancer Charity gala event in Manchester, and it had a Bond theme. I was thinking it would be nice to have something signed by Sean to auction, and asked my friend Gareth Owen in Roger Moore's office if he knew where Sean was. As luck would have it, he was in London and I managed to get a message to him. The next day, a lovely signed photograph of Sean as Bond arrived – and sold for a fortune!

Keeping it in the family

It's funny how things in life have a habit of repeating themselves, and there was no exception in our family.

Kate followed in my footsteps and became an actress, and soon landed the part of Miss Casewell in the long-running Agatha Christie whodunit *The Mousetrap*, which had been playing in London's West End since the early 1950s. It was common practice for the producers to change the cast every six months and, as Kate was nearing the end of her contract, she started looking further afield for work. Her agent offered her an audition for a part in a new film – a new James Bond film! It was, in fact, *GoldenEye* starring Pierce Brosnan. The *Mousetrap* producers were so thrilled with her performance that they offered her a further six-month contract, and in an ironic twist of fate she found out she had also landed the role in *GoldenEye*.

Kate now found herself in a situation very similar to my own over 30 years earlier. Luckily the producers of *The Mousetrap* were far more accommodating than Rodgers and Hammerstein ever were, and her performance schedule was reworked to allow her time out to film.

Sadly, most of Kate's scenes, which were with Pierce in the casino, ended up on the cutting room floor to make way for more action. It's one of those awful decisions an editor and director must make when their running time is too long.

Before the scissors were wielded, Kate's casting generated a lot of publicity. It was all along the lines of 'Her mother helped introduce Sean Connery as 007 and now Kate Gayson is helping introduce Pierce Brosnan as the new Bond.' We both appeared in newspapers and on several chat shows together. Whoever thought of having mother and daughter in the same movie franchise really did hit the jackpot; not that it needed it, of course, as *GoldenEye*, like its predecessors, was another huge success.

In 1998 I was absolutely thrilled to hear that what at the time had seemed like the most difficult line in film history, 'The name's Bond... James Bond,' had been voted *the* most famous line in film history, and I felt proud to have helped Sean deliver it!

Fifty years on, Bond is still part of my life. I have to say it has been an absolute honour to be part of the franchise and its continued success is a true testament to all those who worked in front of and behind the camera. When you work on a Bond movie you become part of a very special family, and it's a family I love dearly.

Chapter Nine

The Swinging Sixties

L ots of people say that if you remember the 1960s you weren't actually there. Well, I never wore flowers in my hair, turned on, tuned in, or dropped out. In fact, all I remember is working damn hard and enjoying every minute of it. Well, almost! Read on...

As you already know, *The Sound of Music* ran from 1961 to 1967. Despite the heavy workload the show placed on our lives, I am quite amazed how many other projects I managed to squeeze in; more on those in a minute. Being in any long-running West End show means your social life is virtually non-existent, but that isn't to say once the curtain comes down we actors all go to bed. Like New York, London was a city that never slept and, as soon as the greasepaint was off, we'd head off to dance the night away or go for dinner at one of London's top restaurants, in particular the actors' favourite haunt, The Ivy.

One night, a gang of us were all eating and chatting quite happily there when an extremely handsome-looking gentleman entered the restaurant, causing all heads to turn. It was none other than film legend Cary Grant, every bit as dashing in real life as he was on screen. It turned out that Cary was dining alone, so we invited him to join us. Happily, the only empty seat was next to me and we got on like the proverbial house on fire. So much so, he asked for my number and promised to call whenever he was next in town and we'd do dinner again. Sure enough, he was true to his word, and whenever Cary was around we'd get together, sometimes even driving down to Bristol to visit his mother.

One day we made a luncheon date at The Ivy and Cary, after looking down the menu, asked if they could do him bangers and mash.

'I'm really sorry, sir, but we do not serve sausages and mash,' the waiter said snootily.

'You don't serve bangers and mash?' he asked, disappointedly.

The Ivy may well be regarded as a place where the stars hang out, but it was also equally well known (and still is today) as a restaurant offering simple, traditional British dishes: fish and chips, corned beef hash, shepherd's pie and the like. Despite his years in Hollywood, Cary was still a real Anglophile at heart and really loved English food. The expression of utter dismay on his face was just too much to take, so I took the head waiter to one side and suggested that one of the staff nip down to Berwick Street market and get some sausages. It took some persuading, and my reminding them who Cary was, but eventually a kitchen porter was dispatched to buy a pound of the best porkers money could buy.

Cary was absolutely over the moon, so whenever he was in town and fancied lunch, I'd book The Ivy and give them the nod to stock up.

Pewter for AL

While tucking in to that first lunch at The Ivy, Cary told me he'd just bought a new house in California and his dining room had a high ledge which he said looked very bare. He thought some old pewter plates would look absolutely perfect along it and asked if I knew anywhere in London that might sell them. So I told him to leave it with me and I'd go up to Portobello Market as, if they were anywhere, they'd be there.

Knowing that if I was recognised the stall holders would undoubtedly hike their prices when I asked how much, I donned

a wig and dark glasses and used as little make-up as possible in
the hope I could fly under the radar and get a favourable deal.
With a strong Cockney accent I went from stall to stall but they
either had nothing suitable or dodgy reproductions at extortionate
prices. I was just about to give up and head home when I spotted
a furtive-looking couple running an antiques stall, and decided to
give it one last shot.

'Excuse me, love, ya wouldn't happen to know where I can get
some pewter would ya? It's for a wedding present and all I've seen
so far is fake,' I chirped.

'Oh yeah, it's all fake, my love,' the lady replied. 'I've got plenty
of that. The real stuff is hard to come by these days.' I thanked her
and, feeling very disappointed, I headed back to my car. 'Excuse
me, love – excuse me, hello?' I heard a voice behind me shouting.

I looked round and it was the lady, waving and beckoning me
back to her stall. 'I've just remembered, love. I'm sure I've got
some pewter in my loft. I don't live too far from 'ere so if you
wanna come and have a butchers when the stall closes you'd be
welcome.' Fine, I thought, but looking at the rest of what they had
to offer, I didn't hold out much hope.

Back at their place I climbed the ladder into their filthy loft, and
my eyes widened as I saw what must have been 30 or more pewter
plates in a tatty old box. Granted, they were absolutely thick with
dust but closer inspection revealed they were indeed genuine.

'How much d'ya want for this little lot love?' I asked.

'£800,' she replied, quick as a flash. I said, 'You've gotta be 'avin
a laugh, ain't ya. There ain't no way I'm paying 800 quid for that.
It's filthy!'

We spent the next 20 minutes haggling and I finally managed
to get her down to £350. 'What an absolute bargain,' I thought
to myself as it must have been worth thousands, but she was
obviously pleased to get shot of it. She asked how I was going to
get it home. I said I'd got an old banger parked around the corner

and I could manage. I'd actually just bought a brand-new car, but of course I didn't want her to see that or I was sure the price would suddenly increase. Thankfully, her son offered to give me a hand with the boxes.

As I was saying goodbye I heard the woman say to her husband, ''Ere Bert, I told ya it was Eunice Gayson.' So much for my disguise!

With the car weighed down, I struggled home at a snail's pace, rushed into the house, grabbed the telephone and excitedly called Cary, who couldn't believe what he was hearing.

'You've got 30-odd items of pewter for £350 each? That's incredible' he said.

'No, I paid £350 for lot,' I replied.

He couldn't thank me enough. What's more, some of the plates had the initials AL on. Archie Leech was Cary's real name and he said the whole thing was fate; he believed he was destined to own that pewter. And, as he'd just finished shooting a movie in Europe, the film company were shipping equipment back to the US and offered to take the pewter along with the cargo.

Cary was so pleased with my efforts he said that when he was dead and buried he'd leave me the pewter in his will. I protested, of course, but he insisted, which I thought was extremely kind of him. From that day on I never heard another peep from him... and I didn't get the pewter when he shuffled off this mortal coil either! Someone somewhere is probably admiring it to this day, thinking how lucky they are to own Archie Leech's family heirlooms.

Saintly encounters

In 1963 I not only got to work with an old chum but a James Bond in the making – Roger Moore.

Producers Robert S Baker and Monty Berman had acquired the rights to the Saint novels by Leslie Charteris and had set up a series with Lew Grade of ITC. I'd worked for ITC before on *White Hunter* and *The New Adventures of Charlie Chan* and, as with the Bond films, felt I'd become part of a family, headed by Lew. He really was quite a character and was responsible for some of the most popular TV shows of the 1960s and '70s, including *Thunderbirds, The Prisoner, Danger Man, Man in a Suitcase, The Champions* and *The Persuaders!* Need I say more?

Having gained permission from the Rodgers and Hammerstein organisation to work on the show, my first appearance was in an episode called *The Invisible Millionaire*, which was shot out at Elstree Studios in Hertfordshire. My West End commitments meant I could only shoot on non-matinée days or, if I was needed for the morning of a matinée day, I was whisked by helicopter to Elstree and back again. Talk about glamorous!

My first day's shooting was an absolute joy. The cast and crew were especially lovely, which in turn created a wonderfully relaxed atmosphere and a real sense of non-urgency, which was quite ironic really as they only had ten days to film each 48-minute episode. Roger was his usual charming self and hadn't lost any of his sparkle or naughty schoolboy sense of humour, which everyone loved.

I returned again to *The Saint* in 1965, guest starring in an episode called *The Saint Bids Diamonds*. This was actually one of the last black and white episodes to go into production and it was written by Norman Hudis, who wrote the early Carry On films.

The budgets were so small that you were often asked to bring your own clothing and jewellery to wear. The wardrobe mistress would go through the script with you, explain what costumes she envisioned and ask you to bring in two or three examples of each, after which the director would have the final say. I naturally brought in my most beautiful clothes, which were instantly dismissed as simply not working when shot on black and white film, so I had to opt for more conservative and plainer colours. Then, when I read in one quite heavy scene that Simon Templar was to rip *my* dress, I wasn't too keen, and asked the wardrobe mistress to back me up. She did so admirably, arguing that her budget was limited enough without losing a dress from her stock. But when she realised it was actually one of my own dresses that was to be damaged, she shrugged her shoulders and thereafter wasn't bothered. How about that? You were never compensated for damage to your own outfits as they figured your appearance fee was reward enough.

Leslie Norman – father of Barry Norman, our favourite film critic – directed one of my episodes. He had a bit of a reputation as a shouter, but he could be equally charming when it suited. There was one occasion when a new script supervisor came on set, quite possibly a trainee. She was in her early twenties and Les kept looking at her, smiling widely. During lunch he sidled over to her and asked her name, then said, 'Would you mind if I call you Spanner?' The young lady looked quizzically at him. 'You see,' he explained, 'every time I look at you, my nuts tighten!'

The Saint's success continued until 1968 when, after 118 episodes, it was felt the series had come to its natural end and it was time to move on. Roger, of course, ultimately went on to be 007, while Bob Baker continued producing and maintained his association with Simon Templar when he brought *Return of the Saint* (starring Ian Ogilvy) to the small screen in the late 1970s.

On 30 September 2009, I heard the sad news that Bob Baker had died.

My thoughts immediately turned back to those fun days out at Elstree, which in reality were over 45 years ago but actually felt like yesterday. One thing is for sure, Bob has left an incredible legacy of film and TV work.

Roger, devastated at the loss of his dear friend and colleague, decided a fitting tribute was in order and on 10 April 2010 I, along with over a hundred others who had known or worked with Bob over the years, descended on Pinewood Studios to celebrate his life and career. I remember looking around the room and seeing many familiar faces. Peggy Cummins, Sylvia Syms, Sue Lloyd, Jenny Hanley, Victor Spinetti, Derren Nesbitt, Valerie Leon, Madeline Smith, Burt Kwouk and Shirley Eaton were all there, as was I, to raise a glass in Bob's honour.

It was an incredibly emotional afternoon, though, sadly, a few notable faces were absent. Roger had been due to fly in from his home in Monaco but his plans were thwarted when all flights were grounded following the eruption of a certain Icelandic volcano. Not even James Bond could get out of that one! Technology saved the day as he called in via Skype to apologise for his absence and pay tribute to his dear friend. Similarly, Johnny Goodman, production supervisor on *The Saint*, was stuck in Tel Aviv and Ian Ogilvy was grounded in LA.

It was a wonderful afternoon and beautifully organised by Gareth Owen and Roger. I just hope Bob was looking down and smiling at all his mates.

Danger! Danger!

Right, let's get back to 1964 and an appearance in another ITC cult favourite – *Danger Man*.

If you remember, I'd worked with a young Patrick McGoohan on *Zarak* in the mid-1950s and even back then he was tipped to be a big star. The producer of *Danger Man*, Ralph Smart, had spotted the young actor in an ITV production of *The Big Knife* and knew he was absolutely perfect for the role of secret agent John Drake. In my episode, I was cast as Louise Bancroft. It wasn't a huge part but, as I always say, there are a million and one actresses just waiting to fill your shoes.

The premise of the story involved Drake being sent to the West Indies to investigate a murder. How exciting I thought; I could almost feel the warm water lapping around my ankles as the sun slowly disappeared over the horizon. When I read the call sheet, the harsh reality hit me. As with most ITC productions, rather than sipping cocktails on a balmy Caribbean beach, I would actually end up gulping down a cup of cold tea in the MGM Borehamwood studio canteen.

I have to admit, meeting McGoohan again wasn't one of the most pleasurable experiences in my life. I'd noticed during the *Zarak* days that he had an air of quiet arrogance about him, but by now he really did take himself very seriously indeed. I'd heard that even before he'd signed on for the role he was calling the shots, demanding dramatic changes to the character. Arrogant or not, he went on to greater stardom in another cult classic, *The Prisoner*; in fact, he wrote and directed quite a few episodes himself, though mercifully didn't ask for me.

October 1965 took me back to Elstree yet again, this time for an appointment with John Steed and Emma Peel aka *The Avengers*, in an episode entitled *Quick-Quick Slow Death*. My character, Lucille Banks, was the principal of the Terpsichorean Training Techniques Inc dance school. Thank God I wasn't cast as the receptionist – having to recite that to every caller would have proved a real mouthful!

It all started off when a dead man was found in an old pram and, after a bit of investigation by Steed and Peel, we discovered that the innocent little dance school was actually a front for a spy infiltration scheme where enemy agents were replaced by anonymous bachelors. Patrick Macnee and Diana Rigg were really easy to work with but they both took it all a bit too seriously. 'Oh come on,' I said, 'lighten up – it's not Shakespeare!' Maybe I'd worked with Roger Moore too much! The cast also included Maurice Kaufmann who, at the time, was married to former Avenger Honor Blackman.

Helping hand

Although my working life was incredibly busy, my dear sister's disability was constantly in the back of my mind. I saw her regularly of course, and she wanted for nothing, but it made me think of those who were much less fortunate than Pat. So I launched myself more and more into charity work, often acting as auctioneer, which, I must say, I actually became rather good at.

At one particular fund-raiser I met Richard Attenborough and his wife Sheila Sim. Dickie mentioned his involvement with the Muscular Dystrophy board and went on to explain that the disease weakens the muscles and gets worse over time, and as there is no known cure it leads to death at an all too early age. He said they were desperate for well-known faces to go out, spread the word and raise funds for the poor boys who literally had a death sentence hanging over them. I volunteered and accompanied Dickie to the Truelove School in Ingatestone; the first thing that struck me was the bravery of the poor darlings. Dickie hoped to take the most advanced wheelchair cases on a trip to Holland, but without funding it was an impossible thought.

At the time I was still in *The Sound of Music*, so had a bit of a profile, and took it upon myself to make their dreams come true and give them a day out they would never forget. With Dickie's help I managed to persuade British Airways to charter a plane from Southend to Rotterdam and I played air hostess to the 23 boys on board. We had a wonderful time visiting the miniature Dutch town of Madurodam and then the 60-acre flower garden in Kirkenhoff.

In the end we were let down by the press, as I don't think they realised the severity of this terrible disease and it was all flowered up as being just a nice trip out for some poorly children. I set out on my own personal crusade to make everyone aware of what these brave boys had to face each day, and as soon as I was out of *The Sound of Music* I travelled the country being interviewed on both TV and radio, trying to raise awareness.

Negatives

I was in Foyle's bookshop on Charing Cross Road when a novel called *Negatives* by Peter Everett caught my eye. I knew it had recently won the Somerset Maugham Award for literature so decided I'd give it a go.

It was a rather odd tale of a couple, Theo and Vivien, who spend their days constantly bickering but then pass their evenings acting out rather bizarre role-playing games, which in turn enhance their lovemaking. Theo, for example, takes on the persona of the serial killer Dr Crippen while Vivien alternates between his wife Cora and mistress Ethel! Problems start to arise with the arrival of another woman, a photographer named Reingard, who suggests Theo take on a new persona, that of World War I fighter ace Baron von Richthofen (aka the Red Baron), which of course threatens his relationship with Vivien.

I know you're thinking it all sounds rather weird but I was quite hooked and thought it would make a terrific film. I decided to make a few enquiries and discovered the film rights were still available, and I snapped them up for £10,000. It was a large sum of money, but I was confident it would work. Initially, I financed everything myself, including hiring Peter Everett himself to write the screenplay, engaging director Peter Medak for his first feature and Glenda Jackson for her first leading role. I felt she had just the right qualities to play Vivien.

Setting up a movie is never straightforward, but it served to add so many more demands on my time, which was limited enough, what with me being on stage every evening and sometimes filming during the day too. In the end, the whole *Negatives* production began to take over my life and, financially, became quite draining. So I decided to sell the project lock, stock and barrel to the Walter Reade organisation in the States, who specialised in projects for art houses and TV outlets. I didn't lose anything in the end, but equally didn't gain much either, other than the experience of turning a novel into a film, and all the trials and tribulations involved.

Negatives was released in 1968 by Paramount Pictures. Along with Glenda Jackson, Peter McEnery was cast as Theo and Sean

Connery's then wife, Diane Cilento, as Reingard. Other notable appearances came from Maurice Denham, Norman Rossington and Stephen Lewis, who of course went on to play Blakey in the long-running ITV sitcom *On the Buses*.

Playing for laughs

I'd appeared in quite a lot of comedy, what with The Goons and revue shows, and in the 1960s I found myself cast in a whole new series of exciting programmes alongside the best of Britain's funny men and women.

First up, in 1961, was the *Bernard Bresslaw and Friends* TV special. Bernie was a huge star after appearing in *Our House*, whereupon ITV decided to give him a shot at his own show. I've worked with quite a few entertainers who were more than happy to hog the limelight – Arthur Askey, anyone? – but not Bernie. Instead, he let his 'friends' take some of the laughs too, which is a real rarity in this business. He was such a generous performer and an absolute joy to work with, and as such everyone wanted to appear in the programme. Libby Morris and I did a rather slick duet in our episode, while Graham Stark and Burda Cann performed a rather bizarre ballet as Popeye and Olive Oyl.

I was later asked, by the BBC, if I was available to appear in a new TV sketch show they were producing called *Before the Fringe*. It took its title from *Beyond the Fringe*, the stage show (written and performed by Peter Cook, Dudley Moore, Alan Bennett and Jonathan Miller) that was considered the forerunner of the satire boom. *Before the Fringe*, on the other hand, was to feature comedy performers who were in vogue before the so-called 'new wave' had swept through the comedy scene. It was written by the likes of Noël Coward and Galton and Simpson, and starred such actors as Beryl Reid, Dora Bryan, Cicely Courtneidge, Ronnie Barker and Joan Sims. I only appeared in a couple of episodes but the old-fashioned style did prove popular and another series was commissioned.

During the shoot of *Before the Fringe* I received a request from Dick Emery, saying he wanted to meet and discuss my appearance in several of his comedy shows; apparently he'd remembered me from revue a few years earlier. He, like Bernie Bresslaw, was so easy to work with but I must say he moved fast. That didn't bother me, however, as I was used to it.

Following *Before the Fringe* I spent a couple of months on the road in the Keith Waterhouse and Willis Hall play *Say Who You Are* with the Australian actor Charles Tingwell, before returning to the BBC once again for an appearance in *The Further Adventures of Lucky Jim*, which was based on the character created by Kingsley Amis, and brought up to date by Dick Clement and Ian La Frenais. Keith Barron starred as Jim Dixon, the misfit Yorkshireman who headed to London and found himself at odds with the big city. The Beeb then kept me on for *The World of Beachcomber*, a surreal comedy show inspired by the then famous Beachcomber column in the *Daily Express*. As in the column, the programme consisted of a series of unrelated sketches, only here with links between them provided by Spike Milligan dressed in a smoking jacket and cap.

Bad luck

By 1968, with *The Sound of Music* over, my social life was beginning to get back on track, and I visited the theatre a lot. How nice it was to sit out front rather than being on the stage! Anyhow, one night after some show or other, I was in the theatre bar and got chatting with an actor named Brian Jackson. To cut a very long story short, it wasn't long before we fell in love and became an item.

Brian was to become very well known in the 1980s as 'The Man from Del Monte' in various television commercials. The tagline of the adverts was always, 'The Man from Del Monte. He says YES.'

In this instance, I wish I'd said 'NO!'

On 21 June 1968, however, Brian became my second husband. I believe everyone makes mistakes in life, this marriage being one of mine. The only good thing to come out of it was our beautiful daughter Kate and my wonderful grandchildren Morgan and Jessica.

As a wedding gift for Brian I purchased a former Anglican Girls School in Hampden Gurney Street, London. Brian had been a photographer in the navy and was keen to set up a new facility in town, and so Hampden Gurney Studios was born. Initially it was let out as a photographic studio but the eventual plan was to use it also for film and TV. Before that became a reality, a Greek musician named Evangelos Odysseas Papathanassiou moved in to the second floor and set up a recording studio. He became rather better known as Vangelis.

After our divorce Brian allegedly sold the studio for £2 million – but I didn't see a penny of that!

Speaking of financial bad luck, I'm reminded of the time in 1966 when I was approached by theatre impresario Martin Landau (not the American actor of the same name) with a proposal to loan him some money in order to prolong his West End production of *Robert and Elizabeth*. It was an operetta-style musical based on the lives of poets Robert Browning and Elizabeth Barrett, with music composed by Ron Grainer and lyrics by Ronald Millar. The original 1964 production at the Lyric Theatre had been a critical success, but further investment was required for it to continue beyond that run.

Buoyed up by the reviews and acclaim, I decided to lend Landau £15,000. But at the last minute the decision was made to use a much smaller theatre than the one we'd discussed, and it was all a disaster. I tried to reclaim some of my money, but it took two years; in the end Landau went bankrupt and my loan was repaid. So with that settled and a new husband on my arm, things seemed to be looking up in 1968. Hah! I was then presented with a tax bill for £5000, which was due as a result of the loan repayment. Talk about injustice!

With all this going on, I nevertheless managed to fit in an extra West End engagement, playing opposite Nicholas Parsons, Joan Sims and Peter Butterworth in Anthony Marriott and Alistair Foot's comedy *Uproar in the House*, staged at that home of farce, the Whitehall Theatre.

It's a girl

Early in 1969, I was thrilled to learn that I was pregnant with our first child. It was such an exciting time for Brian and me. I'd always wanted children but I was so busy with my career that it just didn't happen... until now.

As the due date drew closer I received a call from my sister Pat, who was absolutely beside herself. When I eventually managed to calm her down she told me Mother had fallen down the stairs and had been rushed into Richmond Hospital. We were then living in Hove, East Sussex, and being heavily pregnant I was forbidden to drive. So I rang Brian, who drove all the way home from his studios in London and took me to Richmond. I rushed into the ward and gently took my mother's hand. Her eyes flickered and she slowly turned her face towards me.

'Good, you came. I love you,' she whispered.

'I love you too, mummy, always,' I said.

And with that, her head fell to one side and she slipped away; it was almost as if she had been waiting to see me one last time before she died. I ran screaming to the nurses' station in the hope there was a slight chance that she could be revived, but sadly the nurse confirmed my worst fears. My dear mother was no longer with us. We were absolutely devastated. The greatest tragedy was that she was so looking forward to being a grandmother and had spoken of nothing else for weeks. But she never had the chance of seeing or holding her granddaughter.

I stayed in Richmond with Pat until after the funeral and then returned to Hove to prepare for the arrival of the baby. A couple of evenings later a friend invited me to celebrate her boyfriend's birthday at a dinner party in town. Social occasions were the last things on my mind but my friend was quite adamant, thinking it might be a good tonic for me. The birthday party was in full swing when something most peculiar happened. Oh no! My waters had broken in the middle of an Italian restaurant!

Luckily the boyfriend was a gynaecologist and immediately called an ambulance. I was in blind panic mode by now and remember summoning the restaurant manager to apologise for ruining his banquette. Quite ridiculous, really, when you think I was about to give birth!

'No problem,' he said. 'But if it's a boy please call him Antonio after me. Or Antonia if it's a girl!'

By the time the ambulance arrived the contractions were becoming more and more frequent. Somehow we managed to squeeze out of the packed restaurant without too much fuss, then I noticed the look of horror on the paramedic's face.

'Oh, you ain't havin' a baby, are you miss? I ain't finished me course yet!' he said.

'I don't care. Just tell the driver to put his foot down and get me to the hospital!' I screamed.

The ambulance lurched forward at a fair old speed as the paramedic did his best to keep me calm, though I think he needed the gas and air more than I did. We must have driven for at least 30 minutes before the ambulance screeched to an abrupt halt. 'Thank God,' I thought, but my elation soon turned to sheer horror when the driver informed us he'd taken a wrong turn and was now at the end of a country lane with nothing but a field in front of us.

'We seem to be lost,' he said apologetically.

I was really beginning to lose the plot now and just told him to do whatever was necessary to get me to the nearest hospital. He radioed ahead and requested a police escort to take us to Brighton and Hove Hospital, where the staff, mercifully, were ready for my imminent arrival. I was popped straight onto a stretcher and into the delivery room where my beautiful baby daughter was born.

'At last,' I thought, 'we are now a complete family.' Well, I've always been an optimist!

Chapter Ten

The Not So Swinging Seventies

The 1970s proved to be a very challenging period. Not long after Kate's birth, Brian and I separated, then divorced. It was probably one of the lowest points of my life. I was now faced with being a single mother and a working actress, and while Kate was the absolute light of my life I will freely admit it was a terrible struggle.

My dear mother's passing had left a huge gaping hole. She was the one constant I'd depended on for so many years and had given me so much love, support and encouragement, all of which I now needed more than ever. I made the conscious decision not to take on any major long-term acting projects. But I still had to put food on the table, so I couldn't just sit back and pretend I was reading scripts or considering various projects like some actors do. I had to get out there and work.

At the time, we were still living in Hove and whenever possible I'd take Kate with me to interviews and rehearsals. Of course, everybody absolutely adored her and she never ever caused a fuss – in fact, she usually slept the whole way through. Sometimes it was impractical to take her with me (to a live TV broadcast for example) and for that reason I hired a nanny – not a decision I was comfortable with but I had very little choice. Whenever I'd been away, it would break my heart to come home and hear Kate sobbing her heart out and hearing how much she'd missed me.

One of my first roles in the new decade was Madame Aix in a couple of episodes of the Yorkshire Television comedy series *Albert and Victoria*. It was set in the late 19th century, centring not on the royal family, but Albert and Victoria Hacket. Albert, played by Alfred Marks, ruled the family with an iron fist and enforced strict moral values. I suppose it could be described as a humorous version of *Upstairs Downstairs*. It was so wonderful to catch up with dear Alfred again; we hadn't worked with each other for years.

One final Adventure

In 1971 my agent called and said I'd been offered a part in a new ITC series called *The Adventurer*. Lew Grade was still riding high and had now been asked to produce two 30-minute series for the US market – *The Adventurer* being one.

In it, Gene Barry played Gene Bradley, a wealthy government agent who also posed as a movie star travelling the globe in search of adventure, espionage and intrigue. In the episode *Thrust and Counter Thrust*, Anton Jurzyck – whoever he was, as it was never explained – was kidnapped and locked away in Countess Marie's country home. Of course, I played the Countess, an expert fencer who just happened to be romantically linked to the dashing Gene Bradley – who was also, curiously, an expert fencer. I don't need to tell you where this is going, do I?

I must say it wasn't one of the happiest film shoots I'd been involved in. Barry was a very difficult man to work with, creating a rather tense atmosphere on the set. I was absolutely flabbergasted when one day he questioned the length of my fingernails – which were pretty average by anyone's standards – and remarked how the viewers' attention would be on them rather than him. Can you believe that? I don't think any of my co-stars were too fond of him either.

Having recently produced *The Persuaders!*, which was one of the most lavish shows on TV, this time round ITC scrimped and saved wherever they could, most notably in using 16mm film stock rather than 35mm. So they had more budget, they reasoned, for exotic filming locations. Great, I thought, but, as usual, my hopes were dashed and I didn't leave Elstree! The beautiful view from the roof of my mansion was actually scratchy stock footage of the French Riviera inserted later.

A few years back, I heard a story that Gene Barry had been approached to record a commentary for the DVD release of *The Adventurer* but declined on the grounds that he never made it, even suggesting that they'd got 'the wrong Gene Barry'. 'How arrogant,' I thought, but it was no surprise really. I do have to say, it wasn't the best ITC show by any means so maybe he preferred to forget it. Certainly, after a recent viewing I couldn't believe how cheap it all looked. Not only that, the story seemed rushed and made very little sense. Many critics branded it 'bland and formulaic' – I wouldn't disagree.

The Adventurer was the last time I worked for ITC; they had decided to move away from TV and into making films, producing the likes of *Return of the Pink Panther*, *The Eagle Has Landed* and *Raise the Titanic*. The latter had such a huge budget that Lew Grade said 'It would have been cheaper to lower the Atlantic.' Typical Lew!

Whodunit?

The exact year evades me, but I was touring with a production of *Witness for the Prosecution* in the early 1970s. This was based on an Agatha Christie short story about a dramatic murder trial. It was an incredible part and, though I don't usually blow my own trumpet, I do have to say it's probably one of the two or three best roles I've ever played.

Anyway, at one point the tour hit the Edinburgh Festival. During the summer months, university dorm rooms were always let out to visiting theatre companies as hotels were impossible to find at festival time. One morning, I was leaving my room when the door opposite opened and a woman, smiling politely, said in a very heavy Eastern European accent, 'Good morning. Didn't I see you in the play last night?'

'Yes, that's right,' I said. '*Witness for the Prosecution.*'

'Oh, you were tremendous,' she replied. 'It really is a wonderful play.'

'Thank you so much, that's most kind,' I said. 'Tell me, what brings you to Edinburgh?'

She was studying for a post-grad degree, she explained, and was due to take her final exams the following week. After that she was 'going back to work in the Soviet Union.' We chatted for a few minutes, said our goodbyes and went our separate ways. She seemed very friendly and I thought no more of it until I returned home after the show that night. As soon as I opened my door she came out, obviously looking for someone to chat with. I was a little tired but invited her in for a cup of coffee.

She explained that she really enjoyed talking as it helped improve her English. We nattered for what seemed like hours, during which I happened to mention I'd once hoped to film a series in Russia for ITN, all about British people who had moved there. Despite plans being quite advanced and the Russian Embassy being very co-operative, it all fell through when our interpreter became embroiled with a leading politician's daughter in Moscow! Her interest was heightened, but I was so tired I said 'I really must go to sleep now.'

As she was about to leave, she hesitated and asked, 'Would you like to come to Russia?'

I was quite taken aback. I hardly knew this girl so I smiled politely, said 'Goodnight' and closed my door.

I started to get suspicious when our 'chance encounters' continued, morning and evening, throughout the week. She told me how her husband had links to the Ministry of Culture in Russia and was trying to promote English theatre there. I said it sounded fascinating, but then came the hammer blow.

'I'd be very interested in this production you are starring in coming out to Russia, with you in it.'

'OK,' I said, 'that sounds interesting. But I'll need to discuss it with my director...'

'You might like Russia a lot, you know. I think you'd like to stay there,' she added.

Thinking on my feet, I said, 'Oh no, I have a small child.'

'You can bring her with you! We'd make sure you'd have good accommodation and would get you a place in one of Moscow's top dramatic companies.'

She then went on about it being a wonderful country to bring up a small child in, and how much I'd like the people and their theatres. But everything she said all seemed terribly long term. Anyway, I made enquiries the next day at the university, discovering that nothing was really known about her, aside from her being very intelligent and a great student. However, alarm bells starting ringing when it was mentioned she'd been questioned by the police the previous year, 'but the matter was dropped.' 'What matter?' I asked, to no effect.

I successfully avoided her after that, but when our run in Edinburgh was drawing to a close my Russian neighbour changed tack and became really very pushy. She would come to the show and say she needed to know if I was prepared to visit, and kept on about how she 'needed to know now.'

Trying to brush her off, I replied, 'Oh, I need time to think, it's a big move', with no intention of ever going. I told my fellow cast members, and as a result received a call from someone at the university telling me to 'avoid' my neighbour as it was suspected she was a KGB recruiter. It all sounds so far-fetched, but I assure you it's true and indeed the KGB did recruit through universities, and actors were often targeted as they were able to move around the world quite freely with tours and films. Thankfully, I never saw or heard from her again – or I might now be writing this book in Russian!

The witching hour

I was next approached by Mary Parr, director of the Adeline Genée theatre in East Grinstead (and mother to Melanie Parr, who played one of the Von Trapp children in the stage version of *The Sound of Music*), who was planning to stage a production of John Van Druten's witchcraft spoof *Bell, Book and Candle*. This had been done on Broadway with Rex Harrison and Lilli Palmer, and on film by James Stewart and Kim Novak.

I played Gillian Holroyd, an 'average modern-day witch living in New York City' with her trusty Siamese cat, Pyewacket. The story centres on a handsome publisher, Shep Henderson (played by Simon Oates in this instance), who moves into her apartment building. She, of course, wants him and casts a spell to make him fall in love with her! It doesn't quite go as planned, and she ends up being exorcised.

Mary said that she was having terrible trouble finding a suitable feline to fill the role of Pyewacket, and as we were opening soon it was actually making her quite anxious. I had another of those eureka moments and suggested she 'audition' my own cat, Mossie, a beautiful Persian Blue. I brought him in to the theatre and Mary thought he'd be absolutely perfect. Within a week Mossie was eating out of the palm of my hand and knew all his lines! The added bonus came when he was paid a small fee, which was tax-free.

After *Bell, Book and Candle* I rejoined the old firm for a while and toured in a production of Rodgers and Hammerstein's *The King and I*, playing Anna. Peter Wyngarde was cast as the King Of Siam. He'd opened in the role in the West End in 1973 with Sally Anne Howes as Anna, and after a successful year it hit the road and that's when I was asked to join the cast. Peter had one of the most beautiful velvety deep voices you could ever imagine, and I just fell in love with it. In fact, I got told off during rehearsals quite a few times as I drifted away listening to him, resulting in a couple of missed cues and an angry director!

It was a very happy tour and one which Kate accompanied me on, without ever being any trouble. I used to rehearse my lines and sing the numbers to her in the dressing room; had Kate been a few years older she could have been a stage prompter, as she must have known the script just as well as, if not better than, everyone else.

After that tour I was offered a role as a high-class tart in the Grapefruit production of the Restoration comedy *The London Merchant*; no one can ever accuse me of typecasting, can they? Charting the downfall of a young apprentice after his 'association' with a prostitute, I guess you could say the play was a 'forgotten' masterpiece, as it was rarely performed. We were booked to play the Georgian Theatre Royal in Richmond, North Yorkshire, which had been built in 1788 and was one of the most beautiful theatres I've ever seen. Rehearsals were pretty tough, as there was lots of dialogue to get to grips with, but thankfully the reviews were positive. One critic suggested that the 'avarice and general wickedness' I brought to the part 'added considerably to the enjoyment of the piece.'

With the success of *The London Merchant*, Grapefruit Productions were keen to perform another Restoration comedy, this time *The Careless Husband*, written by Colley Cibber in 1704. I starred with John Stuart Anderson, an acclaimed actor noted for his mastery of one-man shows.

To the manor...

I have to admit, I was now finding life in Hove a little tiresome. It had become a bit too much of a bustling metropolis for my liking and as Kate was due to start school I felt a move to the country and more peaceful surroundings would give us a better quality of life. By chance, I came across an article about the most beautiful manor house in Haslemere, Surrey. I say manor house but it was actually a number of houses, and everyone had an acreage of land. I managed to get Kate into the local village school, where she made lots of new friends and spent many happy hours with them riding horses at the local farm. We had terrific neighbours and if I had to pop up to London for an interview they were always happy to look after her.

However, as idyllic as it all sounds, other circumstances made my life quite difficult. After my marriage breakdown and split from Brian, I faced an acrimonious custody battle for Kate which was reported in all the newspapers. Our divorce didn't go through until 1976 or early '77, so you can imagine the animosity involved in the intervening years. I thought because my divorce from Leigh was relatively civilised this one could be too. Oh boy, was I wrong.

I didn't really appreciate how it was all affecting me, to be honest. Yes, I tried to busy myself as best I could and bring money in. But an incident in late 1974 – in which I believe all my anguish, worry and concern came to a head – proved extremely embarrassing and caused one of the biggest heartaches of my entire life.

While I had kept working in theatre, it was true to say that TV and film work, which paid far more handsomely than stage work, had virtually dried up in the early 1970s. It was no fault of mine; that's just how the business goes. I then learned that my father-in-law, whom I was very fond of, had died suddenly. Kate was beside herself about having lost her only grandfather, and it was just a horrible, horrible period. In October 1974, with Kate's fifth birthday fast approaching, I decided to buy her a new pair of shoes. We headed out to Farnham on a shopping trip but when we arrived the store was closed. I banged on the door a few times but there was no response. It made me feel incredibly anxious and upset, and inexplicably weepy.

The Not So Swinging Seventies

Because Kate had brought a note home from school asking me to buy some brown paint for an art project she was working on, we then walked along the High Street and into Woolworths. Kate immediately asked for some sweets, so I explained we needed to find some paint for her project first. But she was having none of it; she caused a real fuss and literally dragged me towards the pick'n'mix counter. After the upset outside the shoe shop this was something I really didn't need. Woolworths was stifling and packed with shoppers, and I began to feel rather odd. Even now I'm still unsure what really happened. Apparently, I grabbed, not one, but eight bottles of shoe colouring and stuffed them into my bag. Kate was still nagging for sweets so I paid for those and, in a terribly flustered state, left the store.

As I walked out of the door, I felt someone grab my arm. 'Excuse me, miss,' he said assertively. 'Could I see the receipt for those items in your bag?'

I didn't understand what he was saying. 'Items in my bag? What items?' I thought.

In a daze of total confusion, I opened my bag and there was the shoe colouring. I panicked and searched around for the receipt but of course couldn't find it. I apologised profusely and explained I'd had a lot on my mind and that I'd simply forgotten to pay. But he was having none of it.

'I'm sorry, miss. Would you please follow me to the manager's office?'

The security guard told the manager what had happened and the police were called. I was arrested for 'shoplifting goods to the value of £6.61.' Having being bailed to appear in front of the Magistrates, I returned home feeling absolutely heartbroken and desolate. Things were already difficult enough without being publicly humiliated. Of course, the press always love to build you up and then knock you back down, so they had a field day with this.

As the weeks went by there was a constant stream of support from the public, and I received literally hundreds of letters saying how ridiculous the whole situation was. Friends and colleagues were ringing and writing non-stop; they couldn't believe what had happened.

I was summoned to court in December 1974. There I pleaded guilty to stealing the shoe colouring and explained to the magistrate that life had become very difficult since my marriage break-up and that the whole sorry situation was simply a cry for help; something I was just too proud to ask for. The magistrates realised I wasn't a petty criminal and handed me a two-year conditional discharge, ordering me to pay £25 costs. I returned home feeling harassed and totally exhausted, but it had certainly given me a wake-up call.

Thankfully, Christmas afforded me a well-earned rest, which was badly needed. I hoped the New Year would bring an end to this emotionally exhausting period of my life.

Yet more intimacy

I've always looked back very fondly on my early days working in revue, so I was absolutely overjoyed when, in early 1975, Peter Myers asked me to appear alongside Stacey Gregg and Clare Faulconbridge in his show, *Intimacy Takes Place*, at the New End Theatre in Hampstead. After the events of the previous year I just wanted some stability back in my life and, more importantly, some *fun*!

The style was the same as ever, but times had changed. Gone were those skits on American teenagers and the Brontë sisters, and in came our new targets of Women's Libbers, British cars, Margaret Thatcher and the Brits abroad. In one particular number I lost everything but my dignity mid-song; can you imagine that happening in the twee 1950s? I think not!

Staying true to my word I spent quite a lot of that year at home with Kate but I did appear in a play, Jack Popplewell's *Darling I'm*

The Not So Swinging Seventies

Home, at the Theatre Royal Windsor and on tour. Though this one was an unhappy experience, the year ended with more theatre – *Babes in the Wood* at the Cheltenham Everyman.

The following year, a tour of Peter Blackmore's comedy *Miranda* was offered. It was a rather bizarre tale that somehow worked. With a wife who has no interest in fishing, husband Paul Martin heads down to the Cornish coast alone where he snags Miranda, a mermaid. She pulls him deep into her underwater cave and refuses to release him until he agrees to show her London. He then disguises her as an invalid in a wheelchair and takes her back to his home for a month-long stay. His wife, Clare, reluctantly agrees to the bizarre arrangement but on condition they hire someone to look after her, in the form of Nurse Carey.

I'd first played Miranda in the late 1940s, back in the old Richmond rep days. At that time, Ken Annakin's famous film version, with Glynis Johns, Googie Withers, Margaret Rutherford and my future friend Zena Marshall, was still current.

On one particular evening in Richmond I got more than just a bruised ego. It must have been around 30 minutes before curtain-up and my dresser had just poured me into the very tight-fitting mermaid suit. It was absolutely impossible to walk so I'd been assigned a burly guy called Jim to carry me onto the stage around ten minutes before the show started. My dresser went off and I was left with my tail flapping around, waiting. As the clock ticked down to nine, eight and then seven minutes I called down to Fred, the stage door manager, to see where Jim was.

'Sorry, Miss Gayson, I ain't seen Jim tonight,' he said.

I asked Fred to call the stage manager and tell him that under no circumstances should the curtain be raised, as I wasn't in position. Just then, Jim rushed through the door, looking rather flushed; it turned out he'd been down the local pub and had lost all track of time. Quick as a flash he picked me up and carried me fast as he could all the way down to the side of the stage.

When we arrived I heard applause and could see the curtain rising. Fred hadn't bothered to tell the stage manager I wasn't ready, and now I was half-way on stage in the arms of a rather red-faced Jim. He panicked and threw me onto the sofa, centre stage, which was very painful indeed! The audience had no idea what the hell was going but thought it all quite hilarious. I was absolutely furious and screamed for the stage manager to pull the curtain down, which made the audience laugh even more.

Slow dissolve back to the 1970s. This time around they were keen for me to play the wife, Clare, as Aimi Macdonald had been cast as Miranda. I realised that if I played it correctly it could be an absolute scream, as the character was so easy to send up and had lots of comic potential. I made a few suggestions to the director and that's how I played it. We opened on 1 March 1976 in Weston-super-Mare to a packed house and great reviews.

Further on in the tour, the famous film and theatre director Lindsay Anderson came backstage and said I'd given 'one of the best comedy performances I've ever seen', adding, 'The way you played it was very inventive.' I was thrilled that it had paid off, and also absolutely flattered that the legendary Lindsay Anderson was in my dressing room, showering me with compliments!

He looked me in the eye and said, 'Eunice, I can promise you, you'll be hearing more from me. I am going to use you in one of my West End productions. I can see us working together a lot.'

And with that he was gone, and I never saw or heard from him again. That's showbusiness!

Richmond bound

Country living was all well and good, but I realised there is only so much peace and quiet you can take! With Kate approaching junior school age I also felt her education would be better served at one of the larger London schools. In early 1977, I made the decision to move back to London, which didn't really go down too well with

Kate. She loved Haslemere and was hardly ever in the house; there was always so much to do and to explore. I, on the other hand, had to be practical. With the only decent school an hour's drive away, and with all theatre opportunities back in the capital, I said we didn't have a choice.

Kate's hesitation to leave Haslemere weighed heavily on my mind, so I thought of a compromise – Richmond. It's close to London but without all the hustle and bustle, and has plenty of places for a growing girl to explore and visit. I remembered my old rep days and how much I'd liked the Surrey town, and after selling the idea to Kate that's where we moved. I found us a beautiful house by the river and enrolled Kate in the Vineyard School, which had a bit of a village feel to it. Mercifully, Kate absolutely loved it!

Ingrid

I'd known Ingrid Pitt for a number of years and, as she now lived quite close to us in neighbouring Twickenham, our friendship really blossomed. Ingrid had quite an incredible film career, appearing in movies like *Where Eagles Dare*, *The Wicker Man* and a couple of Hammer horrors, for which she is most fondly remembered. One day she told me that she'd formed her own touring company along with her husband, Tony Rudlin, and Robin Ellis, a rich young man with playboy tastes. (Now where had I heard that before?) She explained the company would be called TRIP (so named after her and Tony's initials) and their first production was to be *Duty Free* – a farce written by *Emmerdale Farm* scribe Neville Siggs.

Ingrid asked if I'd like to be involved. At first I wasn't too keen; I'd seen these so-called farces before and half the cast were usually in a constant state of undress. I told her that while I was more than happy to try something a little more, shall we say, sexy, running around the stage in a bra and pants really wasn't my thing. Ingrid assured me that it would be nothing of the sort. It was all set in a country cottage and she was going to play the much put-upon wife with *Space: 1999*'s Nick Tate as her two-timing husband. She suggested the role of nosy neighbour Cynthia Hodges to me, adding that veteran comedy actor Tim Barrett would play my other half. Ingrid also pointed out that she'd hired Victor Spinetti to direct, which was the icing on the cake for me. Well, you can't really get any better than that, can you?

We rehearsed in Richmond and everything was seemingly going fine. I was getting all the laughs in the right places and Ingrid played the straight part really well – maybe too well? You see, I'm not sure what Ingrid said to Victor, but she was obviously worried about not getting many laughs for herself. Anyway, he started messing about with the script and many of my character's funniest lines were cut. I thought it all spelled disaster.

The other cast members said, 'Don't worry, because the character you're playing is still funny.' Well, maybe so, but things came to a head when we opened in Swindon and I *still* got all the laughs, even with my best lines gone! Victor was fired, and two other directors were brought in, one of whom was dismissed after a few days. Ingrid realised that no matter what they did to the play it just didn't work.

Despite its internal problems, *Duty Free* still played to packed houses and was a box-office success. So much so, Moss Empires enticed us to end the tour early and take the play into the West End – to the Victoria Palace, where the play was retitled *Don't Bother to Dress*. Victor came along one night and couldn't believe what had been done – the play was a complete mess. The butchered script and change in directors had had a hugely detrimental effect, and as a result the rather more discerning London audiences stayed away and we closed within five weeks. Poor Ingrid.

I was greatly saddened to hear of Ingrid's death in November 2010. I knew she'd struggled with major health problems throughout her life, but boy was she a fighter! We'd often bumped into each other at autograph conventions and reminisced about the old days; she was such a brave soul and is sadly missed.

Wait Until Dark

On a happier note, in the late 1970s I was invited back to the lovely Weston-super-Mare theatre for a five-week production of *Sextette*, which co-starred Kenneth Connor. I played Marlo Manners, an ageing Hollywood star, who is enjoying her honeymoon with Sir Michael Barrington – husband number six – at the same hotel where one of her ex-husbands is staying. He demands one last fling, or else... and so on, in what was a fairly routine, but nevertheless fun, comedy. It was made into a film that same year, starring Mae West and Timothy Dalton.

More importantly, in 1978 I gave what I consider one of *the* standout performances of my career, playing Susy Hendrix in the Sam Snape production of *Wait Until Dark*.

The plan was to try out for a week at the Planet Theatre in Slough and, if all went well, we'd have the option of a nationwide tour. My friend Barbara Murray had starred in the West End version and warned me that she'd almost had a nervous breakdown doing it! I can quite believe it, as it's actually a terrifying play focusing on the ordeal of a blind girl being terrorised by three crooks who break into her home. In an attempt to stop them I had to do all sorts of things, including pulling all the lights, because of course it didn't make any difference to her. In the final act the auditorium was actually plunged into darkness in order for the audience to share the fear of blindness.

It's a very taxing and tiring play to perform. I played it with my eyes open, but I was unable to react to other characters or visual occurrences on stage – which really makes your performance quite guarded, unless you totally and utterly throw yourself into it. Which I did, wholeheartedly.

The tour was green lit, but I was just so worn out after that first week I barely had the energy to do anything else, let alone think about taking my nine-year-old daughter on the road with me for months, so I bowed out. Nevertheless, I was overwhelmed by the praise my performance generated, including *The Stage* newspaper's assertion that 'Eunice Gayson mastered the problems [of being blind] and gave an exhausting performance which kept the full house on the edge of their seats.'

At the end of a rather challenging decade in my personal life, on a professional level I really couldn't have asked for more!

Chapter Eleven

Into the 90s ... and the Woods

1980 kicked off with an offer to appear in a production of *Kismet* at the Connaught Theatre, Worthing. Donald Scott was starring, and I knew him well because he'd taken over from Roger Dann in *The Sound of Music*; in fact it was Donald who called me about it, and set up a meeting with director Nicolas Young.

Kismet is quite a grand and lavish play, but sadly the budgetary constraints of our production did not extend to much! Though the costumes were very nice, it had the feel of being 'not quite the full Monty' and it didn't go beyond a two week-run. I was very disappointed, to be honest, as it certainly had the scope, albeit with a little extra investment. Heigh ho.

Round about the same time, *The Sound of Music* was revived in the West End before going on a UK tour. I was offered the part of the Baroness but just couldn't commit to a long indefinite run at that point; my priority was being around for Kate, and months on the road was really not an option. Honor Blackman was subsequently cast, I was delighted to hear.

Dracula's daughter

When Roy Hudd called to ask if I'd take part in his afternoon television show *Movie Memories*, it sounded huge fun. Being only a day away, up in Norwich at Anglia TV, it didn't really interfere with family life, and it was such a lovely, easygoing programme. Roy told me their postbag each week was absolutely huge, and that they selected guest stars from the suggestions of people writing in; everyone from Phyllis Calvert, Charlie Hawtrey (in his last ever TV interview), Ingrid Pitt and Diana Dors appeared.

My chat with Roy whetted my appetite to be back in the thick of it, but several years went by before I finally accepted an offer to return. One of our great loves, Kate's and mine, was to vacation in Spain during school and college holidays, and it was during one of our trips, in 1988, that I received a phone call from two guys who had this play called *And Here's Me Without a Gun*. They said they wanted me to play Dracula's daughter, the main female lead.

The zany story centred around two characters, Vanderbilt and Bergdorf (as played by the writers, Lee Harrington and Robin Hope-Johnston), who take a troupe of 26 itinerant singing nuns around the world, all led by Dracula's daughter, who is attempting to get her father a better press. I told you it was zany! It might have been subtitled 'The Sound of Music meets Hammer Horror'.

Anyhow, my character hires the Glitter Glitter club in New York for a visitation from the convent ladies, but on arrival discovers that two members of the Rockettes chorus line (Vanderbilt and Bergdorf) have also booked the club for a reunion. What's more, the barman has arranged to interview that same night for vacancies among his topless waitresses.

I thought it was all very cute, and quite different.

Anyway, we went on this funny little tour. My name still meant something then; not what it did a decade earlier, but it helped bring people in to see the show. Lee and Robin were virtual unknowns and were playing the two guys; it was essentially a three-hander. Although they'd written an interesting script, the show received mixed reviews. In 1993, however, they called me up and said they'd been asked to put the play on again and wondered if I would guest star. It was a five-night run, and the final show was to be a charity performance for the Terence Higgins Trust at the St Martin's Theatre in London. I happily agreed to play Dracula's daughter once more.

In the late 1980s, Kate attended Putney High School, and was doing very well there. They had a theatre group and she joined in, more often than not playing the lead in their productions. Such was the impression Kate left that they now have a bursary in her name.

There was no denying Kate wanted to follow her parents into the business, and, remembering how much my mother had encouraged me, I was more than happy for her to try. Being level-headed (like her mother), Kate, having scored top grades at school, decided she'd apply for university first, getting a degree under her belt before pursuing an acting career. She naturally chose a university which had a big theatrical department and went off to Warwick. Happily, she did very well and gained an honours degree, then opted to take an extra degree at Aston University in Birmingham, again on a course with strong theatre connections.

Upon her graduation Kate joined the National Youth Theatre, and soon afterwards introduced me to a fellow student she was quite sweet on named Jude Law. It seems he's done rather well for himself since!

The wedding singer

In 1990, while I was in Majorca, a friend of mine asked me to sing 'Ave Maria' at a big wedding in Palma Cathedral. I said 'I'd love to' and went along. Now, this just goes to show how quirky life can be. Apparently, a casting director who happened to be there on holiday had wandered in to the church and said, 'Oh, she's still around and still sings beautifully.'

When I got back to London she rang me and said, 'There's this part in Stephen Sondheim's *Into the Woods*; would you like to audition for it?' It sounded fun, and now that Kate was at university I was available for work, so why not? I auditioned for, and got the part of, the Grandmother.

The show was a reworking of several Brothers Grimm fairy tales including Little Red Riding Hood, Jack and the Beanstalk, Rapunzel, and Cinderella, all set around an original story of a baker and his wife and their quest to start a family. Several other well-known Brothers Grimm tales were alluded to and referenced, too. Stephen Sondheim composed the music and the script was by James Lapine.

It was by no means a new production, albeit new to London, as it had opened in San Diego in 1986 and premiered on Broadway a year later, where it won several Tony Awards, including Best Score, Best Script and Best Actress in a Musical (Joanna Gleason). There was then a 1988 US national tour before it came into the West End in London, with a cast including Julia McKenzie, Imelda Staunton, Patsy Rowlands and Nicholas Parsons (whom I'd worked with in *Uproar in the House* in 1968 and *Darling I'm Home* in 1975). I ended up playing three characters – Cinderella's mother, Grandmother and The Giant.

Stephen Sondheim has never really admitted to anyone, as far as I'm aware, what it was really all about, saying that it's for everybody's heart, mind and soul to decide for themselves. For me it was about the end of the world; how the world was going to bring disaster on itself if it didn't change – an unusual concept for a musical but very entertaining nonetheless.

Sondheim came over for the auditions and rehearsals and was very much hands-on. I remember it being an extremely complicated score, with demanding lyrics which weren't easy to learn, but as always we got on with it. My only trepidation was that we were to open without any previews. That's really an invaluable time when, for a week or two before press night and opening proper, the cast and crew can really get to grips with the show, with full costume, audience and orchestra, enabling them to iron out any last-minute glitches.

Into the 90s ... and the Woods

I don't know why we didn't have previews, but certainly Sondheim wasn't very happy about it either, as on the opening night he was very nervous indeed. He'd been to the dress rehearsals, but that's not quite the same as a preview, so to distract him I told him we'd met before in New York at the Hammersteins' house.

'Really?' he said.

So I launched into the story about my Aunt Eunice being their friend, and how she always lent her ear to his new work. He suddenly realised he knew exactly who I was talking about. 'Do you remember a 16-year-old English girl who came to visit?' I asked. 'You were there with Oscar and Jamie, and we chatted about it being my first transatlantic flight.'

His jaw dropped open. He could only have been a young teenager himself. The Hammersteins, through his initial friendship with their son Jamie, really became mentors to Sondheim after his parents divorced, and he learnt at Oscar's knee. It all rang true and he suddenly remembered me from four decades earlier; he became very relaxed and chatty.

He asked about my Aunt Eunice and I told him that she and Lewis had a daughter who was also called Eunice (the family tradition, if you recall?). I also pointed out that I hadn't seen my cousin in years, until recently when somebody I knew in Spain said they'd been to North Africa and met an American woman living in Tangiers who was called Eunice. So I said, 'Do you happen to have her address?' 'Yes,' my friend said. Last I heard, cousin Eunice had married a very well-known Arab doctor in North Africa, so it all clicked. Out of the blue I wrote to her and indeed it *was* my cousin. So I went over with Kate and my brother Kenneth when he was over in the UK on one of his annual trips from Australia. My Aunt Eunice, meanwhile, lived until a grand old age.

Next thing we knew, it was time for curtain up and on we went ...

I never cease to be amazed by the quirks of fate and the coincidences we encounter in life. Who'd have thought that teenage boy in the garden in New York would go on to write some of the finest musicals ever? And who'd have thought that little English girl in the garden would go on to play in one of them?

Anyway, it was a lovely, lovely show and I very much enjoyed working with Julia McKenzie, who is such a wonderful, witty, fun and giving lady. It also whetted my appetite to tackle other things again. Although we ran for less than a year at the Phoenix Theatre, we were nominated for half a dozen Olivier Awards and won two! We knew the Phoenix had been booked the following year and we would need to move to another theatre if we were to continue, but the promoters decided not to transfer as audience numbers were dwindling, so we came off.

I didn't realise, meanwhile, that I'd played the Phoenix before, until one of the cast members said she'd been upstairs and seen a great big poster with my name on it. It was for my stint with the Abbey Players back in the late 1940s, *They Got What They Wanted*. It all came flooding back; I'd quite forgotten about it.

Fitness first

Just before starting *Into the Woods* I was sitting in a café in South Molton Street, London, quietly minding my own business, when I noticed, out of the corner of my eye, the lady at the next table staring at me. She then walked over to the payphone, dialled a number and started talking rather excitedly to the person on the other end, still staring. Finally, after about five minutes, she came over and introduced herself.

'Hello, Miss Gayson,' she said. 'It *is* Miss Gayson, isn't it? My name is Irene Estry and you are my father's favourite actress! Would you be so kind to speak to him on the phone?'

Her father was an absolute delight and I was more than pleased to hear I'd made his day. I asked Irene to join me for coffee and, what seemed like hours later, a new friendship was cemented which is still going strong to this very day.

Into the 90s ... and the Woods

At the time, Irene was, as she still is today, working at Granada Television as a fitness instructor, and she mentioned that she was hoping to produce TV programmes and videos appealing to women and their busy lifestyles. My ears well and truly pricked up. I've always been on the lookout for new challenges and wondered if this could be it? We got our heads together and the ideas started coming thick and fast. Being realistic, however, I was heading into what could be quite a long theatre engagement so I said we'd reconvene when my schedule became a little less hectic and unpredictable.

Slow dissolve to a year later and one of the projects we discussed and felt passionate about was a little-known exercise regime known as Aqua Aerobics. It hadn't really been explored at any length and we felt confident that we were on to a real winner with this one. Health and fitness was all over the television at this point, with Mr Motivator on Breakfast TV and just about everybody, from Jane Fonda to Britt Ekland, bringing out fitness videos. Of course, some of those workouts were quite tough, and if you were of, shall we say, 'a certain age' they weren't really physically suitable, However, Aqua Aerobics was quite different, in that the buoyancy from the water you were in added a dimension of relative ease.

We had quite a bit of interest and eventually sold the idea to a Spanish company who were very keen. Irene developed the workout routines which were to be filmed in South Africa and my commentaries were to be dubbed on later. We were at quite an advanced stage of pre-production, with the cameras and lighting all hired, when disaster struck. I took quite a nasty tumble and the whole project had to be put on hold. Then when we tried to re-group one of the financiers had to drop out and, well, we just couldn't seem to pull it back together. It was a real shame but it didn't stop me working with Irene again. More on that later...

Talent spotting

In 1992 Kate was playing on the Isle of Man, and at the other theatre in Douglas the annual pantomime had been announced as *The Wonderful Wizard of Oz*. I'm not quite sure how it came about, or who had a word in whose ear, but the next thing I knew I was offered the role of the Good Fairy in the show. As Kate was going to be there over Christmas, I thought it would be a fun way of spending the season together. So I trod the boards once more and had an absolutely brilliant few weeks.

As you already know, a year later, Kate landed a role in the long-running Agatha Christie play *The Mousetrap*. That, plus her part in *GoldenEye* and lots of voiceover work, enabled her to buy her own flat in Richmond. I like to think I always let Kate get on with it, and that I supported her without adding pressure or pushing her in directions she didn't want to go.

Along with supporting Kate, I've always been the type of person who likes to nurture new talent, so when I was told about a girl singer a friend of mine had discovered in Spain I was intrigued. The next time I was over, I was taken to a tatty little hotel where the singer was in cabaret. Well, despite the less than auspicious surroundings, she was everything I'd been told; fabulous-looking, with a brilliant voice and huge personality. What's more she spoke nine different languages. Let's call her Isabella.

I made it clear that I wasn't an agent, but I thought she had a great future ahead of her, and the more I spoke to her the more I felt she had the X-factor. Isabella said, 'I would love to come to London. Could you introduce me to a few people?' I thought, 'Yes, I could do that. I know a few agents and promoters.'

We chatted further and then she landed me with, 'My boyfriend told me I should be under contract, so will you offer me one?'

I said, 'Hang on, I'm just talking about making introductions!'

'No, I trust you and want you to represent me. I don't want to come to London and have no one to promote me.'

Into the 90s ... and the Woods

Well, it was all rather sudden and very unexpected on my part, but I really thought this girl could go places with a bit of help, so I called my lawyer and asked if he could draw up a simple agreement between us. I must admit, I worked like crazy on her behalf and called in favours everywhere. In her first week she played the River Club on the Thames (which was the most exclusive dinner-dance club in London), then I got her into the Pizza on the Park, and following that I secured her a gig at a club which was opening in Richmond.

But, you know, after just these first few performances I noticed an attitude problem setting in. Isabella didn't know anything about the River Club or Pizza on the Park and didn't realise they were very good bookings that a lot of singers would kill for. She never once said thank you; it was as though she expected it all just to land in her lap.

Then trouble started. She was staying with me in my house in Richmond, and I walked into her room one day to see all the furniture piled in the corner. 'I don't like it, it's not my taste,' she said. She then accused me of spying on her and trying to manipulate her. Me? Her so-called manager was trying to manipulate her? I'd actually succeeded in getting Isabella onto a TV talent show and taken her shopping to buy different outfits (spending a fortune, I might add). But she thought she knew best. Just to be bloody-minded, she decided against a song I'd suggested, which I'd had written for her and which I felt would show off her talents best. She chose instead a crappy cabaret song. So what with that and the tarty outfit she chose to wear I thought she'd blow it. Talent will out, however, and she came back saying it was between her and another girl.

I was beginning to think maybe I'd been a little hasty and should have given her more say. But then I discovered that, rather than pay her appearance fees into a bank account I'd set up for us, she would ask for cash on the night and had no intention of paying me a commission. A commission that, in any case, wouldn't be anywhere near enough to cover the huge expenditure I'd incurred. We'd had a deal and I'd stuck to my part, so I told her to pack her bags and get out. She was gobsmacked. I said she was totally unprofessional and, as talented as she was, she could now 'Forget it.'

Isabella said she didn't need me because she'd had an offer to go to Japan, which she'd been negotiating secretly; as far as she was concerned, I didn't figure any longer. Anyhow, I later heard the Japanese job was a sham and that she'd gone back to Spain with her tail between her legs. That taught me a big lesson and I vowed never to get involved in that side of the business again.

Mind you, I've said that about so other many aspects of the business. On one occasion in the late 1970s a management wanted to change the terms and conditions of our contracts in a show, and we were all up in arms over it. The rest of the cast asked me to represent them in the negotiations, like a sort of shop steward, and I accepted on one condition – 'that you all stand by me, because I'll never work for this manager again if I do this and I don't want him to point the finger at me as a lone troublemaker.'

I realised then that actors will always let you down. When the manager refused to negotiate, they all said that it was my idea and sided with him! Another valuable lesson learnt the hard way. I should just keep my head down and remain quiet.

Anyway, back to 1993. My eyes were beginning to cause me trouble and I was diagnosed with glaucoma. I had to give up driving for a start, so I decided to semi-retire from the business. Well, do actors ever retire? But that's not to say other opportunities didn't arise...

Chapter Twelve

Bond is Back!

It was around the end of 1993 when I received a letter from an enthusiastic young man named Gareth Owen, who was then a 20-year-old physics student in North Wales with ambitions to help revitalise the ailing British film industry. He'd persuaded the management of Pinewood Studios to let him take over the complex for a day in April 1994 to host 'British Film Day' and focus some attention on what we do best in Britain. I was struck by his passion, commitment and achievements and readily agreed to attend.

I subsequently heard him on BBC Radio 5 Live one evening talking about the film day, and when asked what he'd like to do after graduation he said, 'I think I'd like to be a film producer.' 'Interesting,' I thought, 'I'm looking forward to meeting him.'

Anyhow, 9 April 1994 arrived and I headed over to Pinewood and met up with the other guests, including Sylvia Syms, Liz Fraser, Burt Kwouk, Walter Gotell, Bryan Forbes, Nannette Newman and Julian Glover, to name but a few. I had a lovely long chat with Gareth, who mentioned he'd been given a film script (by Walter Gotell, in fact) and thought it had the makings of a good story, but he didn't really know what to do next or where to go with it. I felt he needed a bit of a mentor, and I volunteered to give him the benefit of my experience; after all, I'd been involved in the business for most of my life and knew all the pitfalls and problems. So, following the success of film day, Gareth took an office at Pinewood and set up a production company. He often popped over to Richmond to see me with his business partner to chat about all things film and television over lunch.

My daughter Kate's career as an actress was beginning to take off and, as I mentioned earlier, she was cast in *GoldenEye* with Pierce Brosnan. Well, every girl should do a Bond film, I say!

I was invited to the press and cast screening of *GoldenEye* with Kate on the morning of the premiere, at the Odeon Leicester Square. We were, in fact, among the very first people to see the film and to see Pierce Brosnan as the new James Bond; what a terrific Bond he made, too. Afterwards, Planet Hollywood hosted a special lunch where I was reunited with Norman Wanstall, who had been the sound editor on *Dr No* (and who later won an Oscar for the same job on *Goldfinger*) after more than 30 years.

Towards the end of the decade Gareth phoned and said he was writing an official history of Pinewood Studios, and would I share a few memories? Would I? Try and stop me! In May 2000 his book, *The Pinewood Story*, was published by Reynolds & Hearn and a launch party was arranged at the studios one sunny afternoon. It coincided with Gareth unveiling a special memorial stone to Desmond Llewelyn, who had died so tragically the previous December. Although I never shared screen time with Desmond in the Bond films, I did get to meet him later on and found him an absolute gentleman, so very unaware of his own fame and popularity. I was asked if I would join Bert Luxford (who made all the Bond gadgets) in unveiling the stone and planting a memorial tree. I was honoured.

Back on the road

Next thing I knew, Gareth asked me if I'd ever considered attending an autograph convention. 'A what?' I asked. How anyone could organise a convention around people signing autographs I never knew, but sure enough it was a big fixture on film fans' calendars. Gareth took me up to the NEC in Birmingham for what was a really eye-opening experience, and yet another re-introduction to the magical world of 007.

The NEC halls are like vast aircraft hangars, not dissimilar to film studio stages, and I was astounded by the sheer number of stalls, tables and people contained within. There were rows upon rows of dealers selling DVDs, games, toys, books, props, masks, costumes and film-related clothing. Then there was a whole area given over to 'autograph signings'. These few rows of tables were laid out, and there was I with *Dr No* and *From Russia With Love* posters behind my chair.

'This is going to be a quiet day,' I thought, but no sooner had the doors opened than I had a queue of people all wanting my autograph, and all wanting to ask me what it was like working with Sean Connery, and if I had a favourite line in the film. In fact, they often quoted lines to me hoping I'd remember the responses! I was absolutely bowled over by the affection, kindness and praise the many hundreds of people gave me. And they came from all over the globe, from the USA to Japan and Sri Lanka.

I was a bit new to it all, and turned to look at a fellow actor sitting nearby. 'Is it always like this?' I asked.

'Yes, but you've been particularly popular,' he replied.

For about six hours solid I signed autographs, posed for photos and answered questions. It was like the 1950s and the Rank film festival visits all over again! Though I was absolutely shattered by the end of the weekend, I'd had huge fun and was treated royally. Who'd have thought there'd still be so much interest in Bond four decades on? But that was just the tip of the iceberg, let me tell you.

In 2001 Gareth helped organise a season of Pinewood films at London's Barbican Centre, kicking off with *Dr No* – what else? I was asked to introduce the film and, along with legendary production designer Sir Kenneth Adam and Bond effects guru Bert Luxford, took to the stage to share a few memories of the movie. From then on I received a steady flow of invitations to attend screenings, conventions and autograph shows all over the UK and Europe.

Of course I couldn't do everything and go everywhere but I must tell you one of my favourite trips (I did it twice in successive years, actually) was to a wonderful film convention in Heerlen, in the Hook of Holland. There were four or five of us 'Bond girls and guys' in the party and we all assembled at Waterloo Station in London to take the Eurostar to Brussels and then connect to local trains into Holland. It was like a travelling rep company. Over my two trips I was joined by Zena Marshall, Joe Robinson, Tania Mallett, Albert Moses, Thomas Wheatley, Mollie Peters and John Moreno. I don't think we stopped laughing, on either trip, from the moment we left London to our return a few days later.

It was all organised by a lovely chap named Kees Blokker and the convention itself was held in a huge football stadium where people from all over Holland, Germany, Belgium, Italy and beyond arrived to collect autographs, have a chat and take some photos. During our lunch break we were served a wonderful gourmet meal in the executive restaurant; I happened to comment I liked the cup and saucer, and asked if the restaurant manager knew the company that made them as I'd love to buy some. Well, the next thing I knew he arrived with a box for me saying it was his gift. You won't believe it, but he'd packed a four-piece place setting of plates, bowls, cups, saucers and cutlery. I could hardly refuse it, but oh dear, how could I tell him I only wanted a single cup and saucer?

When we arrived in Brussels to board the Eurostar the others all went ahead through the X-ray machines and metal detectors. I, on the other hand, was stopped by a rather puzzled security officer who wondered why I had a complete dinner service and cutlery in my hand luggage, all wrapped up carefully in my underwear. Well, what could I say? 'It's a gift from a fan.'

Gareth's business partner Andy Boyle, who travelled with us to look after me, has become not only a good friend but also, with Gareth, my agent. We've travelled together to gigs all over the country, have huge fun and laughs along the way, and have certainly met some interesting people, who, on the whole, have been delightful.

40 years on

In the year 2000 a chap named Dave Worrall contacted me to say he was the UK producer of the 'definitive documentaries' for the Bond DVD releases, and one in particular, called *Inside Dr No*, for which he hoped I'd be willing to be interviewed. It was quite a big affair and they'd pulled together the majority of the surviving cast and crew from the movie, all excepting Sean, who declined to be involved.

As always, it was fun to share a few memories, but little did I realise this was a mere taster of what was to come two years later. 2002 marked the 40th anniversary of James Bond. There was a new film on the horizon with *Die Another Day*, but before that kicked off at Pinewood Eon Productions organised a press conference on 11 January to launch the 20th adventure, followed by a special lunch at the studios for Bond alumni. I was picked up in a limousine and arrived at the studio to meet Pierce Brosnan, Judi Dench, Halle Berry, Ken Adam, Barbara Broccoli, Michael Wilson and Dana Broccoli, among many others. It was a huge, starry occasion and one I was delighted to be part of. I sat next to the managing director of the studios, Steve Jaggs, and half-way through lunch he turned to me and apologised.

'This food is truly awful,' he said. 'I'm so embarrassed.' I'd been far too polite to say anything before, but he'd no doubt seen me attacking the rubber chicken with all my energy. There was a time when film industry catering was the best in the world; after all, a hungry crew do not deliver their best work. Pinewood's catering was run by a franchise company, and I'm pleased to say their licence wasn't renewed the following year.

A group photograph followed, along with a few interviews, before I was delivered home again at what was really the beginning of a hugely busy year, including a special 20-window 007 display at Harrods in London, convention appearances and, in November, the Royal premiere of *Die Another Day*. Unlike anything I'd ever seen before, the Royal Albert Hall in London was dressed as a giant ice palace, mimicking the villain's HQ in the movie, and converted into a 5000-seat cinema auditorium. It was a terribly swish affair with a red carpet running the length of Kensington Gore, and absolutely jam-packed with photographers. Everywhere I turned flashes went off, and fans were hanging over the barriers proffering photos to be signed.

Inside, while awaiting the arrival of Her Majesty the Queen, we were able to watch the excitement unfold on a large closed-circuit screen. It was to mark not only the opening of the 20th film in the series, but also the coming-together of four of the five 007 actors: George Lazenby, Roger Moore, Timothy Dalton and the (then) present incumbent in the role, Pierce Brosnan. Wow!

There was an equally glitzy post-premiere party across the road in a specially constructed marquee in Hyde Park. I spotted Shirley Bassey, Maud Adams, Guy Hamilton, Lewis Gilbert and many more familiar faces. Around the same time, I appeared in an ITV documentary entitled *Best Ever Bond*, hosted by Roger Moore. It was basically a countdown of the most famous and popular Bond scenes, and I was delighted to see that the casino sequence in *Dr No* was in the top ten. I think it'll always be up there in any and every chart!

Along with the TV programme I was interviewed for magazines *Empire* and *Total Film*, just about every national newspaper and all sorts of other periodicals too numerous to mention. It was a little overwhelming in fact.

Kate meanwhile decided to put her acting career on hold after meeting, falling in love with and marrying a lovely young chap named William. They made such a terrific couple and decided to set off travelling the world. Their adventure ended up in America for a while, but they later came back to London to start a family – and their two wonderful children Morgan and Jessica came into our lives.

One day, about six or seven years ago, Kate said she felt the children would have a better life away from the UK, and quite frankly, who could blame her? Having spent many years holidaying in Spain, and living there for a little while in the 1980s, Kate and William decided they'd like to move out there and settle the children into the Mediterranean lifestyle before they started school, when the upheaval would have been twice as difficult. I knew I'd miss them hugely, but it was a move undertaken for all the right reasons.

Happily, William soon found employment in Gibraltar, just over the border from their apartment, and Kate became an English teacher. Their two children settled into Spanish life with relish, and are now totally bi-lingual. I enjoy spending extended holidays over there with them, and always look forward to their trips back to London, too. Without doubt, their lives are absolutely joyous in Spain, with terrific education, wonderful sunshine, clean air, healthy living and a much warmer climate. I sound like an advertisement!

Return of the Saint

In October 2006 Roger Moore invited me to Elstree Studios to join him at a reception where a plaque was unveiled in his honour, celebrating his years at the studio filming *The Saint*, when it was then part of the Associated British Picture Corporation (ABPC) complex.

I remember Roger saying, 'When I was last here in the studios I had a lot more hair, and I had 20:20 vision and a 32-inch waist. Life has caught up with me!' That's just typical of Roger, and, after thanking everybody for coming, he added, 'I'm grateful for this plaque. It's going to be moved to Borehamwood High Street, which was used all the time in *The Saint*. It was meant to be the Champs Elysées, but all they did was flip the film – they forgot about the London buses. I just want to be assured that it will be high enough that dogs can't reach it, because the critics have been doing that to me for years.'

I'm sure you'll be familiar with The Osmonds? Well, I certainly remember little Donny Osmond and his 1970s hits such as 'Puppy Love', but in 2007 he turned his hand to hosting a British TV quiz show called *Identity*, which was in fact adapted from a US format. I received a call asking if I'd be interested in being a guest on the show, which filmed up at BBC Manchester.

In the quiz, a contestant has to correctly guess the real identity of 12 people on numbered podiums, from the available job titles on a screen. Of course, my identity was 'the first Bond girl'. The young contestant looked at the category board, which had only a few identities remaining, then looked at me and asked, 'Could you be the landlady of a B and B?' We were asked not to react in any way, but I nearly fell off my podium when I heard that. 'He must stay at some glamorous guest houses,' I thought to myself. In the end he guessed correctly, though, and I had to deliver the rather corny line 'You have a licence to kill.' Donny asked, 'Was that the film you were in Eunice?' He ought to have fired his researcher!

You know, over the years, I've spoken at lots of events, dinners and fundraisers and I'm always surprised and delighted when someone tells me they enjoyed what I had to say. Taking it a step further, a number of friends, plus my sister Pat, started nagging me to write my stories down and think about putting on a proper one-woman show. The more I thought about it, the more it appealed, as I had so many stories I'd not yet told, let alone the ones people always asked me to repeat.

'OK,' I thought, 'I will.'

Bond is Back!

I called Gareth and Andy, and they kindly fixed up a try-out for me, at the Royal Academy of Dramatic Art in their small theatre there. Around 60 or 70 friends, family and fans filled the auditorium one Saturday evening and *Fried Ants in the Kasbah* was launched – the title coming from my experiences on *Zarak*. I really enjoyed the 90-minute show, and it's always good to play to an audience as you get a feeling for what works and what needs working on. The plan was to fine-tune the act and hit the road, and in fact I had a call from P and O Cruises asking if I'd consider being a guest on one of their trips and perform my show.

However, my darling sister Pat's health took a turn for the worse. She'd been so brave throughout her life and was dealt a pretty rum hand at times. Despite being told she'd never walk again after her childhood illness, she did. She later found love and married, and, despite being told she should never have children, due to the weakness in her bones and spine, which could prove fatal to her, she overcame the odds and gave birth to a son, John. However, Pat was widowed very early on and was absolutely devastated. But with a young child to support and care for she immediately took a job as a secretary to a theatrical agent, and then in later life became involved with the local social services in Richmond.

In the early 1990s we were told the awful news that Pat had leukaemia. John gave up his job to become her full-time carer. Pat underwent treatment and fought so hard. Despite long spells in hospital, constant blood transfusions and an increasingly frail frame, she always bounced back and took a very positive attitude. John was an absolute tower of strength to her, and I visited as much as I could. My plans to take my one-woman show on the road were shelved as I concentrated on being there for my sister.

Pat's condition never really improved, but she was remarkable at adapting and making the best out of any situation. Later, and despite being wheelchair-bound, she took up pottery and became a real whiz. Then she took up oil painting, becoming very accomplished at that too. 'Is there nothing my dear sister can't turn her hand to?' I wondered.

Bonding with friends

Bond, of course, kept popping in and out of my life and the next big milestone was the 100th anniversary of Ian Fleming's birth in October 2008. All sorts of things were planned, from book reissues and exhibitions to a collection of Royal Mail stamps being issued and a huge, huge celebration at the London Palladium on 5 October, entitled *The Story of James Bond*.

Director Dougie Squires called and asked if I'd be part of a 'Bond girl' line-up on stage. 'Sure,' I replied, not thinking much more about it.

En route to the Palladium I called in at Zena Marshall's town house in South Kensington, as we were going to go up together by car. Neither of us really knew what was expected of us, or what the event would turn out to be, but there was a great sense of excitement in the air.

Well, let me tell you, our taxi couldn't get anywhere near the Palladium; there were crowds everywhere. In fact they must have been five or six deep. As Zena and I got out of the car a hundred yards or so from the stage door, we heard the call go up, 'Look, it's Eunice Gayson!' And with that we were surrounded by autograph hunters. 'And Zena Marshall!' someone else called, which brought even more people upon us, all proffering photographs to be signed.

'I think this is rather a big event,' I said to Zena.

We managed to push through to the stage door and saw all sorts of friendly faces, Roger Moore and the newest Bond, Daniel Craig, among them.

Zena and I shared a dressing room with a few of the other girls, and rather eerily the door had '*The Sound of Music*: Dressing Room 1' on the outside. Fortunately, I wasn't expected to perform for

Rodgers and Hammerstein that night, as Andrew Lloyd Webber's sell-out revival was fully cast and enjoying a night off!

The evening was amazing. Hosted by Stephen Fry and Joanna Lumley, it consisted of readings by Jeremy Irons and Toby Stephens, plus interjections from Roger Moore, Daniel Craig and us Bond girls. It was a very special and totally unique occasion. Better still, ticket sales and fundraising from a capacity crowd raised £90,000 for the British Heart Foundation. We were all left shaken and very much stirred.

In the eye of the beholder

2009 marked my return to TV, of sorts, when my dear friend Irene Estry became involved in an episode of ITV's long-running *Tonight* programme, entitled *Age Before Beauty*. The producer, Neil Barnes, asked her if she knew anyone 'of a certain age' who was still attractive, had a healthy positive outlook on life and, more importantly, had resisted the urge to go under the surgeon's knife in an effort to retain a youthful image. Irene suggested little old me; well, who else? (Don't answer that!) My attitude has always been to live life for the moment, and not once have I ever considered any kind of surgery, because as long as I am happy within myself that's all that matters. Perfect, they thought!

Irene had concerns over women's self-esteem and the pressure of remaining youthful, whatever the cost. So, along with *This Morning*'s resident psychologist Emma Kenny, she devised the 'Think It, Click It' campaign. One hundred women aged between 35 and 69 were given clickers and asked to register the number of times in a week when they felt negative about their body image. One of the women involved was actress and *Loose Women* regular Sherrie Hewson. She'd had a face-lift four years earlier but was still unhappy with her appearance, all the more so as the years progressed.

Over the seven days the average result for the 100 women was 252 clicks, but Sherrie Hewson clicked 1400 times. Quite astonishing statistics when you think about it. In the programme, Sherrie and I talked about her image and how she felt so negative about herself, despite being a warm compassionate woman with a face full of character – and I told her so. I spoke with Sherrie quite a lot after that, and kept hammering home how lucky and attractive she was. I saw her on an episode of *Loose Women* recently and was so pleased she was being more positive about herself.

After our show aired, we were all told by Neil that plans were afoot for *Age Before Beauty* to become a series, following the progress of the women over the coming weeks and months. I was asked to present and Irene was asked to help the women make lifestyle choices to improve their self-image. We opened a bottle of champagne to toast our new working relationship, but soon afterwards a call came through telling us that the programme team in Manchester (apart from the producer, Neil) were being made redundant and our planned series had been scrapped. How about that for bad timing?

To this day, Irene and I still come up with ideas for programmes. Maybe one day we'll get around to making one, who knows?

A year to forget

In her 1992 Christmas Day message, the Queen described her year as having been an 'annus horribilis'. Looking back, I've had a few of those myself but nothing would prepare me for 2010… and beyond.

Firstly, I received news from Australia that my brother Kenneth had gone into hospital for what was supposed to be a fairly routine operation, but the surgeon who operated saw that Kenneth was riddled with tumours – he had advanced cancer. The prognosis was not good, and he was given a very short time to live.

Although we lived at opposite ends of the world, Kenneth visited London every year and we remained very close through letters and phone calls. It was a terrible blow, and one which came at a time when Pat's health had taken a turn for the worse.

Bond is Back!

She was told that her heart had been affected by the leukaemia and subsequent treatment, and that she needed surgery to fit a pacemaker in order to regulate it. The procedure was straightforward enough, but the promised improvement after surgery simply wasn't there.

I then received the terrible news that my dear brother Kenny had passed away. I really could not imagine how things could get any worse than they already were.

After visiting Pat one Sunday I decided to call in to my local supermarket in Richmond to pick up a few groceries. Unknown to me, the floor in one aisle was wet and as I walked down I slipped and... When I opened my eyes people were looking down at me asking if I was OK. I felt a searing pain in my left arm and hip, but it seemed the staff were more preoccupied with apportioning blame than calling an ambulance. I was eventually whisked off to hospital with a dislocated shoulder and several broken bones.

Weeks later, after proving myself reasonably mobile, I was discharged. To cut a long story short, I was advised to take legal action, as not only was I out of circulation for weeks, I also had to pass up an offer of lucrative acting work which my new agents Gareth and Andy had set up. However, it was all really a waste of time as, quite coincidentally, they said, the store's CCTV was switched off that week, so there was no record of my fall. Realising I was about to embark on a David and Goliath lawsuit, I decided life was too short and the stress was something I just couldn't cope with.

Pat had meanwhile taken a turn for the worse after her second pacemaker began to falter. She was taken to hospital and connected to all manner of machines to keep her body working.

Previously, I had decided to spend Christmas with Kate, William and my grandchildren in Spain; to get away and rest in the warmer climate would be a huge tonic, my doctor said. I told my nephew John to call me if there was the slightest change in his mother's condition and I'd fly back. Although slightly subdued, we managed to spend a reasonable Christmas together before I returned to London. My first port of call was to see Pat – still being kept alive by life support.

It was absolutely heart-breaking to see my dear sister connected to all this machinery and I knew in my heart of hearts we were nearing the end. My worst fears were realised when the doctor informed us that little more could be done and it would be best to turn off the machines that were keeping her alive. It was one of the most heart-wrenching decisions we'd ever had to make, but we had to be realistic and agreed it would be the best thing to do.

As the machines were turned off, my darling sister opened her eyes one last time and then slipped away into a deep, peaceful sleep. Losing a loved one is hard on anyone, but when a twin loses his or her sibling it is particularly painful, and for the first time in my life I felt totally bereft and numb.

The day of the funeral arrived. I say funeral but as Pat never really had any kind of faith she'd left strict instructions that it should be a Humanist ceremony. Apparently, these are becoming quite popular, catering for those who didn't have any religious views and affectionately celebrating their lives. And what a life to celebrate!

The ceremony was held at East Sheen cemetery and was a small gathering of close family and friends. As we entered the chapel, I heard this beautiful voice emanating from the speakers. I knew Pat loved jazz and thought it must have been Ella Fitzgerald or the like. I turned to John and asked who was singing.

'It's Pat,' came his reply.

I was absolutely stunned. I couldn't believe it. I knew she'd had some singing lessons but never to this standard and I'd certainly never heard these recordings before in my life. John said he'd discovered them while going through some of her things. As we left the chapel they played another song Pat recorded entitled 'Don't Miss Me When I'm Gone', which was very beautiful and hugely poignant.

Bond is Back!

Birthday greetings

In April 2011 I was invited to attend a celebration of Sir Ken Adam's 90th birthday, which was being held at the Royal Institute of British Architects and hosted by BAFTA. I was delighted to accept, but was wary because it was my first public outing since my accident and indeed since Pat's funeral.

Then I received an SOS from Roger Moore. Roger had been filming in Bulgaria and, on the penultimate day, tripped over a cable on the soundstage. That was all fairly harmless but, in an attempt to save him, three electricians (or 'hairy-arsed sparks,' as he preferred to say) all dived down, and in so doing ended up falling on top of him, thus pulling down a light which was attached to the other end of said cable; it landed on Roger's leg. Unable to walk, Roger bravely completed his scenes before being whisked away to hospital in Switzerland via private jet. There they operated on his leg, attached a skin graft and, worse still, operated on his kidneys where stones had been dislodged. So, poor Roger (who was to be the guest of honour) was incapacitated and asked if I would take a letter along to read on the night.

How could I refuse?

I read the letter over several times to myself, and when I was invited to the stage I like to think I delivered Roger's witty missive pretty well, with laughs in all the right places. Great. Well, it was until we all slipped upstairs for a drink after the amazing tributes to Ken, when a young assistant director apologised and said my radio microphone had not been switched on and 'Would I mind awfully doing it again?' I went back downstairs and did my best, but there was no laughter, no interaction with the audience and it all fell rather flat.

So, words of wisdom from Eunice: never go shopping where the CCTV is switched off and never give a public speech until you know they've checked your radio mic at least three times!

I was next asked to star in a couple of short films, one for students at Royal Holloway College and another, more avant garde, production for an art student in south London, all about conceptual artist Lee Lozano. I have always enjoyed helping students and young filmmakers and that extends to young actors too.

A good friend mentioned to me that she'd seen a school production down at Hampton, and was bowled over by a young actor named Chris Yeates, who was about 16 then. Anyhow, she asked if I might have any words of advice for Chris, so I invited him to tea. I was mightily impressed by him, his enthusiasm and his excellent manners; quite the opposite to Spanish Isabella! So much so, I made a phone call, set up a meeting and got him signed up with an agent. While still completing his education, he's gone on to do some work on film and TV and is now a part of the prestigious Yvonne Arnaud Youth Theatre in Guildford. I believe there are big things in store for Chris.

Five decades on

2012 is a special year for London with the Olympics coming to town. It's also a special year for cinema with the 50th anniversary of 007. In fact, this year's BAFTA awards ceremony kicked off with Sir Tom Jones singing *Thunderball* against an on-screen montage of clips from the 22 films... including a snippet of yours truly. With a new Bond film, *Skyfall*, in production and with such a prestigious anniversary looming I had a feeling I might start getting busy – not least with writing this book!

In early January, the phone rang. 'Eunice, are you available to open the 'Bond in Motion' exhibition at the National Motor Museum in Beaulieu?'

'Yes, sure. When and where do they want me... ?'

Britt Ekland, Jenny Hanley, Madeline Smith and I duly performed the honours and ended up speaking to the press, I kid you not, for a solid three hours of interviews.

And so on I go; James Bond never really goes away...

Chapter Thirteen

I Admire My Luck...

I've been hugely fortunate in my career, and I believe talent, hard work and a little luck are all responsible. But 'the harder you work, the luckier you get', I say.

Fairly recently a girlfriend of mine, who teaches theatre at a London college, needed some time off and asked me to cover for her over a couple of days. It was very interesting to meet excited newcomers who felt destined for a career in the business I love so much. After my initial chat, someone asked, 'Please Miss Gayson, what do I need to do to become famous and a star like you?'

I was horrified. 'You don't decide if you are going to become famous; the public decides,' I replied. None of them had actually thought of that!

'What about *The X-Factor*? If I won that I would become a star,' said one.

'Yes, and the public vote, don't they?' I replied.

'Oh yeah...' she said.

'Why do you want to be a performer?' I asked.

'Erm, because, erm...'

'Because,' I interrupted, 'I want you to say, "It's the only thing I can think of, the only thing I want to do, and I feel so excited when I perform." That's the answer I'm looking for. Not "Because I want to be famous," that's for sure. You should strive for success rather than strive to be famous; they are two distinctly separate things and as an actor you should not crave fame alone. You've got to have talent, sure; and if you have talent then you need to develop it and gain experience. Though some people are said to be born with a natural talent, a look etc, it's useless unless honed and guided.'

'Well, how do I get experience?' another asked.

'By taking every single job or audition that's offered to you! Never turn anything down because you never know who you might meet or where it might lead. You can't lose a reputation because you haven't got one yet,' I said. 'Never be late to auditions or on set; you need to build a reliable reputation. You should never, ever, lose heart and learn to live with rejection because for every job you get you'll be turned down by at least nine others.'

The whole class was shell-shocked. It's not what they wanted to hear.

'The fact of the matter is,' I continued, 'you're all here because your parents can afford to pay the fee. I don't know what talent you have before I see your work. Just because you or your family think you're talented isn't enough.'

I'm sorry if I sound brutal, but the surge of talent shows on television, and so-called overnight celebrity, has proven toxic to this business in which I grew up, and in which I grafted as an assistant stage manager, then in repertory and fringe shows, long before I ever thought of getting a film or TV break. Nowadays everyone wants to be on the box or on the big screen!

I told the students again to take everything that was offered to them, no matter if it was out of their comfort zone or wasn't glamorous. I said, 'Never turn down a job because you've not done something like it before. Do research, talk to someone and never to be too proud to ask for help and advice. Seasoned actors will be only too happy to help you.'

Of course things are different now, I know that, and there are so many more actors than when I started out, but you know what? There are always so many talented actors out of work, and there are so many people who leave drama school only to opt out after the first year as they get frightened by all the rejections. The business has never changed in that respect and students need to be acutely aware of it.

'But,' I concluded on my final day, 'if I could chase my dream and be successful there is no reason you can't. Be determined, work hard and always be on time.'

Of course, a modicum of fame is rather lovely too, but I wasn't going to tell them that!

Speaking of 'fame', I recently came across a few fan letters in a folder while looking for something else. Well, not so much fan letters as correspondence, shall I say. They were all from a chap in London who kept writing to me throughout the '00s. They're actually rather amusing as the poor guy confuses me with just about everybody else. For example, he says he loved me in *Genevieve*, thought I was brilliant as Jessica Fletcher in *Murder, She Wrote* and, what's more, he believed me to be the very first Betty in the music hall act Wilson, Keppel and Betty. That'd make me about 102 by my reckoning! Please!

However, bless him, it did make me reflect on how fortunate I have been, with so many wonderful opportunities, and how when people come up to me and thank me for giving them hours of pleasure through my film, TV and theatre roles that it is I who should be thanking *them*. The warmth and affection I feel at conventions is overwhelming and I really do feel that, throughout my life and career, I have been blessed to be surrounded by a loving family, good friends and some very talented and kind co-stars, directors and producers who've made it all possible. Yes, I've been very lucky.

I was so fortunate to have a mother who encouraged and helped me, a loving sister who, despite her own problems, was always there for me, and a wonderful daughter and two adorable grandchildren who make my life complete. Of course, I'm remembered and am – dare I say it? – famous primarily for being in two James Bond films. Not that I mind. But I've done a heck of a lot more too, as this book testifies.

Oh! Excuse me, there goes the phone again.

'Yes, sure. When and where do they want me... ?'

'Hollywood? The Turner Classic Film Festival, to introduce *Dr No*? Well yes, of course.'

With my well-travelled suitcase packed, I headed off to Los Angeles this last April for the week-long festival with my old friend Peggy Cummins (who was there to introduce a screening of *Gun Crazy*). We were treated royally with first class travel, a top hotel suite and a driver at our disposal. So of course we took a ride around our old Hollywood haunts, many of which had been replaced by shiny new office and apartment buildings. It's certainly all changed.

The opening night party was a very swish affair, with Liza Minnelli present to introduce a newly restored version of *Cabaret*, and I rubbed shoulders with my old pals Larry Hagman, Kirk Douglas and Robert Wagner. What a night! To a capacity audience I introduced *Dr No* a couple of days later, and then took part in a Q&A with the lovely Maud Adams, to discuss our lives as Bond girls.

I returned home somewhat jet-lagged, but exhilarated! Oh, there goes my phone again, excuse me...

FILMOGRAPHY

I have tried to be as accurate as possible in listing my work below, but over 60-odd years I've forgotten the odd title and character name here and there, and despite my best endeavours to research the productions, a few details might be missing. Answers on a postcard please!

FILM

Meet Me At Dawn (1946)
Director: Thornton Freeland
Role: (uncredited)

It Happened in Soho (1948)
Director: Frank Chisnell
Role: Julie

My Brother Jonathan (1948)
Director: Harold French
Role: Young Girl

Melody in the Dark (1948)
Director: Robert Jordan Hill
Role: Pat

The Huggetts Abroad (1949)
Director: Ken Annakin
Role: Peggy

To Have and To Hold (1950)
Director: Godfrey Grayson
Role: Peggy Harding

Dance Hall (1950)
Director: Charles Crichton
Role: Mona

Down Among the Z Men (1952)
Director: Maclean Rogers

Miss Robin Hood (1952)
Director: John Guillermin
Role: Pam Wrigley

Street Corner (1953)
Director: Muriel Box
Role: Janet

Dance Little Lady (1954)
Director: Val Guest
Role: Adele

Out of the Clouds (1954)
Director: Basil Dearden
Role: Penny Henson

The Last Man to Hang? (1956)
Director: Terence Fisher
Role: Elizabeth Anders

Zarak (1956)
Director: Terence Young
Role: Cathy Ingram

Light Fingers (1957)
Director: Terry Bishop
Role: Rose Levenham

Carry On Admiral (1957)
Director: Val Guest
Role: Jane Godfrey

The Revenge of Frankenstein (1958)
Director: Terence Fisher
Role: Margaret Conrad

Hello London (1958)
Director: Sidney Smith
Role: herself

Dr No (1962)
Director: Terence Young
Role: Sylvia Trench

From Russia With Love (1963)
Director: Terence Young
Role: Sylvia Trench

The Disappearance of Dylan Jenkins (2011)
[short film]
Director: Lucy Haig
Role: Anwen

Monologue (2011)
[short film]
Director: Jessica Tsang
Role: Lee Lozano

TELEVISION

Halesapoppin (1948)
Company: BBC
Role: Guest

Consider Your Verdict (1948)
Company: BBC

Lady Luck (1948)
Company: BBC
Producer/Director: Michael Mills
Role: Faith

Pink String and Sealing Wax (1949)
Company: BBC
Producer/Director: Kevin Sheldon
Role: Emily Strachan

The Director (1949)
Company: BBC
Producer/Director: Kevin Sheldon
Role: Katie

Dick Whittington (1949)
Company: BBC

Alice (1950)
Company: BBC
Producer/Director: Kenneth Buckley

Here Come the Boys (1950)
Company: BBC
Producer: Walton Anderson

Treasures in Heaven (1950)
Company: BBC
Producer: Kevin Sheldon
Role: Carol Benson

Mother of Men (1950)
Company: BBC

Producer: Eric Fawcett
Role: Jenny

**BBC Sunday Night Theatre
– La Belle Helene** (1951)
Company: BBC
Producer: Eric Fawcett
Role: Leoena

Kaleidoscope (1951)
Company: BBC
Role: Sally in *Alibi*

Nine Til Six (1952)
Company: BBC
Director: Tatiana Lieven
Role: Judy

Goonreel (1952)
Company: BBC
Producer/Director: Michael Mills
Role: various

**BBC Sunday Night Theatre
– Arms and the Man** (1952)
Company: BBC
Producer: Eric Fawcett
Role: Louka

Kaleidoscope (1953)
Company: BBC
Producer/Director: Douglas Moodie

Men of Mystery (1954)
Company: BBC

The Grove Family [episode 17]
(1954)
Company: BBC
Producer: John Warrington

**Stryker of the Yard
– The Case of the Bogus Count**
(1954)
Company: Republic Productions
(Great Britain)
Director: John Krish

**Douglas Fairbanks Jr Presents
– Johnny Blue** (1954)
Company: Douglas Fairbanks
Productions
Director: Lance Comfort
Role: Milly

**Douglas Fairbanks Jr Presents
– The Apples** (1954)
Company: Douglas Fairbanks
Productions
Director: Lance Comfort
Role: Micky

**Douglas Fairbanks Jr Presents
– One Way Ticket** (1954)
Company: Douglas Fairbanks
Productions
Director: Lawrence Huntington
Role: Dolly

**The Vise – Death Pays No
Dividends** (1954)
Company: Danziger Productions
Director: David MacDonald
Role: Julia

**Douglas Fairbanks Jr Presents
– The Mix-Up** (1954)
Company: Douglas Fairbanks
Productions
Director: Tony Young
Role: Angela

The Vise – Blind Man's Bluff
(1955)
Company: Danziger Productions

Director: Paul Dickson
Role: Valerie Dyson

**BBC Sunday Night Theatre
– Whiteoak Heritage** (1955)
Company: BBC
Director: Barry Delmaine
Role: Louisa

**Douglas Fairbanks Jr Presents
– The Thoroughbred** (1955)
Company: Douglas Fairbanks
Productions
Director: Harold Huth
Role: Nora Kenealy

The Vise – The Bargain (1955)
Company: Danziger Productions
Director: David MacDonald
Role: Angelia Clifton

**Douglas Fairbanks Jr Presents
– Mark of the Scorpion**
(1956)
Company: Douglas Fairbanks
Productions
Director: Barry Delmaine
Role: Louisa

Alfred Marks Time (1956)
Company: ITV

**BBC Sunday Night Theatre
– What the Doctor Ordered**
(1957)
Company: BBC
Producer: Alan Chivers
Role: Madame Caprice

**White Hunter
– This Hungry Hell** (1957)
Company: ITV (ITC)
Director: Joseph Sterling
Role: Thelma Thomas

Educated Evans (1958)
Company: BBC
Producer: Eric Fawcett
Role: Lady Fanny Kostaki

Duty Bound
– Tales of a Revenue Man (1958)
Company: BBC
Producer: Adrian Brown
Role: Arlene

The New Adventures of
Charlie Chan
– The Hand of Hera Dass (1958)
Company: ITV (Television Programs
of America Inc / ITC)
Director: Leslie Arliss
Role: Yasmin Rachid

The New Adventures of Martin
Kane, Private Investigator
– The Heiress (1958)
Company: ITV (Associated
Rediffusion) (Towers of London / Ziv
Television Programs Inc)
Director: Cliff Owen
Role: June Hartley

Bresslaw and Friends (1961)
Company: ITV (Associated
Rediffusion)
Director: J Murray Ashford

The Saint
– The Invisible Millionaire (1963)
Company: ITV (ITC)
Director: Jeremy Summers
Role: Nora Prescott

Danger Man
– Man To Be Trusted (1964)
Company: ITV (ITC)
Director: Peter Maxwell
Role: Louise Bancroft

The Saint
– The Saint Bids Diamonds (1965)
Company: ITV (ITC)
Director: Leslie Norman
Role: Christine Graner

The Avengers
– Quick-Quick Slow Death (1966)
Company: ITV (Associated British
Corporation)
Director: James Hill
Role: Lucille Banks

Before the Fringe (1967)
Company: BBC

The Dick Emery Show (1967)
Company: BBC

The Further Adventures of
Lucky Jim (1967)
Company: BBC
Producer: Duncan Wood

The World of Beachcomber (1968)
Company: BBC

Albert and Victoria
– The Gothic Church (1970)
Company: ITV (Yorkshire Television)
Director: John Nelson Burton
Role: Madame Aix

Albert and Victoria
– The Lovers' Quarrel (1970)
Company: ITV (Yorkshire Television)
Director: John Nelson Burton
Role: Madame Aix

The Adventurer
– Thrust and Counter Thrust (1972)
Company: ITV (ITC)
Director: Paul Dickson
Role: Countess Maria

TELEVISION AND FILM
personal appearances

Designed for Women (1947, BBC)
The Teen-Age Show (1948, BBC)
Spring Review (1948, BBC)
Designed for Women (1949, BBC)
Designed for Women (1950, BBC)
Bride and Groom (1953, CBS)
Guess My Story (1954, BBC)
Festival Time (1955, cinema
  featurette)
Gaumont British News
  – British Stars Go to Venice (1955,
  Gaumont British)
Guess My Story (1955, BBC)

Palais Party (1956, ITV)
I've Got a Secret (1958, ITV)
Find the Singer (1959, ITV)
What's My Line? (1960)
World of Sport (1965, ITV)
Movie Memories (1985, ITV)
This Morning (1995, ITV)
Inside 'Dr No' (2000, MGM)
Best Ever Bond (2002, ITV)
Identity (2007, BBC)
The Tonight Programme
  – Age Before Beauty
  (2009, ITV)

THEATRE

Ladies Without (1946)
Venue: Garrick Theatre, London

Aladdin (1946)
Role: Princess Luvlee
Venue: Grand Theatre, Derby

Richmond Repertory Theatre (1947)
- The Barretts of Wimpole Street
- Little Women
- Born Yesterday
- Miranda

They Got What They Wanted (1948)
Venue: Phoenix Theatre, London

The Wonderful Wizard of Oz (1993)
Role: Good Fairy
Venue: Gaiety Theatre, Isle Of Man

The Kid from Stratford (1948)
Venue: Winter Garden and Princes Theatre, London

Goodnight Vienna (1949)
Venue: Folkestone

The Wife Jumped Over the Moon (1949)
Role: daughter
Venue: Richmond Theatre, London

The Lonely Heart (1951)
Role: Lindsay Thatcher
Venue: New Lindsey Theatre, London

Hobson's Choice (1951)
Role: Vicky Hobson
Venue: Grand Theatre, Blackpool

Ring in the New (1951)
Role: various
Venue: New Lindsey Theatre, London

The Irving Revue (1952)
Role: various
Venue: Irving Theatre, London

After the Show (1952)
Role: various
Venue: St Andrew's Hall, Edinburgh

Over the Moon (1953)
Role: various
Venue: Casino Theatre, London

More Intimacy at Eight (1954)
Role: various
Venue: New Lindsey Theatre, London

Oh Men! Oh Women! (1956)
Role: Myra Hagerman
Venue: tour

Born Yesterday (1957)
Venue: tour

Let Them Eat Cake (1959)
Role: Liz Pleydell
Venue: Cambridge Theatre, London

The Little Hut (1960)
Role: Lady Susan Ashlowe
Venue: Playhouse Theatre, Western-Super-Mare

Night of 100 Stars (1960)
Role: herself
Venue: London Palladium

Night of 100 Stars (1963)
Role: herself
Venue: London Palladium

Night of 100 Stars (1964)
Role: herself
Venue: London Palladium

The Sound of Music (1961-67)
Role: Elsa Schraeder
Venue: Palace Theatre, London

Say Who You Are (1967)
Venue: tour

Uproar in the House (1968)
Venue: Whitehall Theatre,
London

The Grass is Greener (1971)
Venue: tour

Witness for the Prosecution
(1972)
Venue: tour

Bell, Book and Candle (1973)
Role: Gillian Holroyd
Venue: Adeline Genée Theatre,
East Grinstead

The London Merchant (1973)
Role: Sarah Millwood
Venue: Georgian Theatre Royal,
Richmond, North Yorkshire

The King and I (1974)
Role: Anna
Venue: tour

Intimacy Takes Place (1975)
Role: various
Venue: New End Theatre,
London

Darling I'm Home (1975)
Venue: Theatre Royal, Windsor
and tour

Babes in the Wood (1975)
Venue: Everyman Theatre, Cheltenham

The Careless Husband (1975)
Venue: Georgian Theatre Royal,
Richmond, North Yorkshire

Miranda (1976)
Role: Clare Martin
Venue: tour

Duty Free (1977)
Role: Cynthia Hodges
Venue: tour

Don't Bother to Dress (1977)
Role: Cynthia Hodges
Venue: Victoria Palace Theatre, London

Wait Until Dark (1978)
Role: Susy Hendrix
Venue: Planet Theatre, Slough

Kismet (1980)
Venue: Connaught Theatre, Worthing

And Here's Me Without a Gun
(1988)
Role: Dracula's Daughter
Venue: Secombe Centre, Sutton

Into the Woods (1990-1991)
Roles: Cinderella's Mother,
Grandmother, Giantess
Venue: Phoenix Theatre, London

And Here's Me Without a Gun
(1993)
Role: Dracula's Daughter
Venue: Secombe Centre, Sutton

Index

Picture
Acknowledgements

Unless otherwise stated, all pictures are from the author's collection.
We gratefully acknowledge the following additional sources:

Back flap
Portrait by Nigel Trigwell.

Picture section one
Page 3: (top) *The Teenage Show* © BBC Television.
Page 4: (bottom left) *Dance Little Lady* © Renown Pictures Corporation.
Page 5: (top) *Out of the Clouds* © Studiocanal Films.
Page 6: *Zarak* © Columbia Pictures Corporation (main photo by Göran Krantz),
The Last Man to Hang? © Columbia Pictures Corporation,
Carry On Admiral © Renown Pictures Corporation.
Page 7: *The Revenge of Frankenstein* © Columbia Pictures Corporation.

Picture section two
Pages 1-2: *Dr No* © Danjaq LLC and United Artists Corporation.
Page 3: (top) *The Saint* © ITV Studios International.
Pages 3-4: *From Russia With Love* © Danjaq LLC and United Artists Corporation.
Page 5: (top) *Danger Man* © ITV Studios International,
(bottom) *The Avengers* © Canal +.
Page 6: (top and bottom left) *The Saint* © ITV Studios International.
Page 7: (top) *GoldenEye* © Danjaq LLC and United Artists Corporation.
Page 8: (top) © Rex Features,
(bottom) © The National Motor Museum.

Any errors or omissions will be corrected in future editions.